Your Key to
OPEN HOUSE SUCCESS

Go From Unlocking Doors to Unlocking Unlimited Leads, Exponential Database Growth and Neighborhood Dominance

SHANNON ENSOR

Your Key to Open House Success

By Shannon Ensor

Copyright © 2015 by Shannon Ensor.

Printed in the United States of America

First Printing, December 2015

ISBN: 978-0-9970862-0-1

Jands Publishing
1 Peter 4:10

www.ShannonEnsor.com

⇨⇨⇨⇨⇨⇨⇨⇨⇨⇨⇨⇨⇨⇨⇨⇨

Your Key to Open House Success is accompanied by FREE online resources!

Visit:

www.ShannonEnsor.com/yktohs/resources

to receive your FREE tools and guides!

⇨⇨⇨⇨⇨⇨⇨⇨⇨⇨⇨⇨⇨⇨⇨⇨

Table of Contents

Introduction..i

{Chapter 1} Real Estate Trivial Pursuit.............................1

{Chapter 2} The Power of the Open House 7

{Chapter 3} Top 10 Excuses Agents Give........................17

{Chapter 4} Mechanics of a Successful Open House........49

{Chapter 5} Day #1 - Tuesday...61

{Chapter 6} Day #2..85

{Chapter 7} Day #3..91

{Chapter 8} Open House Day!..101

{Chapter 9} After the Open House 129

{Chapter 10} Open House Duties for Listing Agents.....139

{Chapter 11} The More the Merrier................................145

{Chapter 12} Safety First...151

{Chapter 13}Implementation Equals Success................155

INTRODUCTION

Chances are pretty good that if you're reading this you are a real estate agent. Or, perhaps you are in the real estate business in another avenue, such as a loan officer, and want to pass along valuable information to the agents you have built relationships with. Either way, I know that you are here to learn how to increase your business and ensure that your real estate career is a successful one.

Your time is important to me. I promise not to write you a book filled with fluff and feel-good statements that lack real-world implementation strategies. I feel that if I do not provide you with useful tips and a new way of thinking, your time is wasted. That is why on almost every single page of this book you will find success strategies that you can begin implementing *today*. I'm also going to point you online to some handy guides and templates (for free!).

You know from the cover of this book that this is about one topic: open houses. While this seems like a narrow topic, you will find how this leg of your business bleeds into others, such as your database, online presence and farming. I want to give you all the knowledge I have on this subject so you can walk away feeling confident and having learned new strategies to boost your business exponentially.

I've honed my open house success strategies over years of doing multiple open houses every weekend. I was deemed the Open House Queen in my office and by other colleagues. I can directly correlate a huge chunk of commissions earned and repeat business to open houses. I am a true believer that open houses are an integral part of your success as an agent.

Through the years, I've further fine-tuned my open house skills through teaching other agents my success strategies. I've garnered information from them, and other agents I work with, about what works and what does not work in open houses. More importantly, I've learned the reasons why agents are not successful at open houses and how they can overcome their failures. I'm going to share all of this information with you so you can become a better agent, too.

Whether you are fresh out of licensing school or a seasoned veteran, you will find this book highly instrumental in your real estate career. I will teach you that while open houses are not the sole way to run your real estate *business*, they are a key component to keeping a balanced career.

Notice the word *business* emphasized above. Brokers, team leaders, and solo agents alike need to understand this is a *business* that you are running. Like any other business, you need to have goals and plans of action to achieve success. A balanced business prevents you from putting all your resources into one leg, while leaving others weak.

By the time you are finished with this book, your open house business will be stronger than ever. You'll attribute closing after closing to open houses, leaving you more time to work on the other areas of your well-balanced business. I'm excited for you, so let's get started!

CHAPTER 1

REAL ESTATE TRIVIAL PURSUIT

Open houses. Some agents love them; many agents hate them.

What's the difference between these two sets of agents? One set has learned how to *properly implement* open houses and sees them as an integral piece of their balanced business. The other set has failed to put a system into place that turns their open houses into closings. This second set of agents has typically experienced a few unsuccessful open houses, deems them a waste of time and decides to take open houses out of their business equation. They are now left with an unbalanced business.

Several elements make up the real estate *business equation* referenced above. To be a well-rounded agent with an ever-growing database that churns out closings and referrals, you must utilize all of these elements.

I'm reminded of my family's favorite game while I was growing up: Trivial Pursuit. In order to win, you had to have all the pieces to your 'pie'. In real estate, if you are missing one of the pieces to your pie, you cannot win – you cannot succeed.

Real Estate "Pieces of Pie"

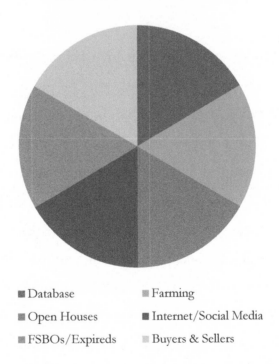

■ Database   ■ Farming

■ Open Houses   ■ Internet/Social Media

■ FSBOs/Expireds ■ Buyers & Sellers

If an agent focuses only on a few pieces of their 'pie', they will become lopsided in their business. Spending all your time and money on internet leads? You are going to have an uneven business that could fail as soon as your internet leads drop off. Likewise, if you ignore open houses as an income source, you will have a hole in your business.

Missing Piece

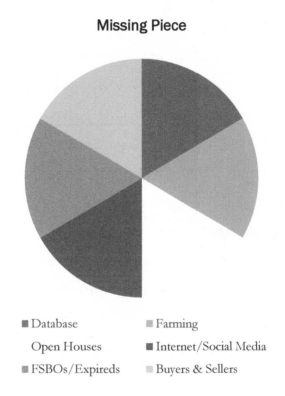

■ Database   ■ Farming

    Open Houses   ■ Internet/Social Media

■ FSBOs/Expireds   ■ Buyers & Sellers

The goal is to have a well-rounded business by *completing* your pie.

Please understand that the use of the word completion above doesn't mean that you can do something once in real estate and expect it to churn out closings for you forever. To be successful, you will need to **diligently** and **routinely** work on your pie pieces for the *remainder* of your real estate career.

I think back to our family games of Trivial Pursuit. My father and brother were huge sports fans so they always went for their orange pie pieces first. Lacking sports knowledge, I strategized to avoid landing on those orange spaces and would save the orange pie piece for last. I'd work on the other five pieces of the pie while they were too busy showing off their sports expertise. I hoped that by the time I'd have to go for the orange piece, I'd be so far ahead, I'd have time to come across a sports question I could answer correctly; or by the time I ever had to go for the orange piece, someone else would have won the game, sparing me from embarrassingly answering 'Michael Jordan' to a football question.

Do you see the hardship and failure in both situations? Avoid open houses, overcompensating your time in other areas hoping to get lucky, and you'll leave yourself with an unbalanced business and ignored source of income. Refuse to learn how to have an effective open house, and you'll experience failure every time.

Take note that I am not saying to *only* do open houses. This, too, would cause an imbalance. While my father and brother were too busy showing off their sports knowledge, my mom and I were sweeping the board in all other categories. We would've made a power team if we could've joined forces, but that's not how the game is played. In real estate, you are your power team. You are responsible for achieving success by creating balance in *all* aspects of your real estate career.

Realizing that open houses are a *must* in your business, you now need to make sure you know how to do them the right way – meaning you will make money and earn repeat business from open houses. By the time you are finished with this book you will have all the tools you need to become successful at *every single one* of your open houses.

Key Notes:

⇨ Properly implemented open houses are a crucial part of your well-balanced business.

⇨You must diligently and continuously utilize open houses – just like any other 'piece' of your real estate business – or else you will be left with gaps that will cause you frustration and loss of income.

CHAPTER 2:

THE POWER OF THE OPEN HOUSE

Every time I speak with agents about open houses, and I mean E-V-E-R-Y-T-I-M-E, I'm presented with excuses. Behind the excuses is a sense of uniqueness – as if that agent has been handpicked for failure when it comes to open houses. They'll say, "open houses never work for *me*."

These are also the agents that come to me later complaining about a lack of business.

I will go over the list of excuses in my next chapter. But, for now, we are going to go with my favorite: "No one came to my open house last week! They just don't work."

This signals to me that the agent clearly does not understand the purpose of the open house. They stop at Merriam-Webster's dictionary definition of an open house: "an event in which anyone who is interested in buying a particular house, apartment, etc., is invited to go inside and look at it."

Think the purpose of an open house is to appease sellers? Wrong again. Open houses extend past looking busy in front of your sellers. When implemented correctly, they are a powerful avenue for increasing *your* business.

The success-driven purposes of open houses are to:

⇨ receive leads

⇨ grow your database

⇨ increase your neighborhood credibility.

Awakened to how impactful open houses can be to the growth of your business, you begin to do more than simply stick a key in the door and wait for people to come to you. You now view each open house as a business-building event and you desire to perform to your best ability because your success depends on your participation.

Side note: open houses *are* beneficial to sellers and listings because they provide valuable marketing exposure.

> The purpose of an open house goes beyond simply opening a door and letting people in.

I've seen open houses sway buyers who were on the fence about purchasing now or next year, because it allowed them to come into the home in a non-committal manner and fall in love with it. Their decision went from wavering to "I gotta have it!"

Open houses also give homes pivotal exposure to buyers who have been searching online too narrowly. Perhaps your listing never came up in a buyers' online search because it was 50 square feet below their desired minimum. Driving around on Sunday afternoon, those same buyers see your directional signs and decide to venture into your open house. They fall in love with what turns out to be the perfect floor plan for their family – something they may have never realized if it weren't for your open house.

Open houses are indeed a necessary element to marketing the home for sale and giving it the optimal exposure it needs. When properly utilized, open houses are equally rewarding to the agent and to the seller.

Open Houses: The Ultimate Multi-Tasker

Open houses serve dual purposes: to give the house extra exposure and to help you grow your real estate career.

We took a look above at how open houses provide great marketing exposure for the home. Now it's time to dive into the success-driven purposes of open houses, which again are: leads, database growth and neighborhood credibility. Remember, these are all crucial to increasing your number of closings each month.

Leads

Open houses provide you with a pool of potential buyer leads *and* seller leads in both the short term and long term. That's right, I said seller leads!

At each open house, you are hoping that a buyer will walk through the door at any minute, fall madly in love with the home, and want to write an offer on the spot. That's one source of a lead you find at an open house.

But, only one person can buy the house, correct? So, your next source of open house leads is from buyers who may not love this particular home, but are ready, willing and able to purchase another home. Your hopes with this type of buyer lead is that they do not have a buyer representation agreement with another agent, and they'd like to employ you to help them purchase the home down the street – or across town in another neighborhood they find more suitable. Simply put, your plan of action is to get one client ready to buy that (open) house and dozens of other clients ready to buy the next available inventory.

Please recognize that seller leads also *flow* from open houses – and in a bit, I'll show you methods to get those seller leads to flow abundantly in your direction.

Ever heard of a nosy neighbor walking through an open house? If I had a dime for every time an agent complained to me that their open house visitors were only nosy neighbors, I wouldn't be writing this book. I'd instead be sipping on a Mai Tai somewhere in Hawaii, thankful for all those dimes that rolled in from complaining agents. Roll the money in your direction instead by seeing nosy neighbors as potential sellers.

Okay, yes, perhaps a small percentage of nosy neighbors are bored and looking for cookies to eat in other people's air-conditioned homes; but build the right relationship with them and they can turn into excellent referral sources for you!

The likelihood of meeting a potential seller at an open house is so great, I always set aside time after an open house to do a pre-listing appointment. You'll find more on this and other seller lead strategies in the chapters to come.

Another subject we will discuss later is how to gain leads through your open house advertising, even when the people do not come to your open house.

Database Growth

Here we see some overlapping because your buyer and seller *leads* from an open house will be entered into your *database*. Even those nosy neighbors – the ones who ate all your cookies and told you they plan to live in their home until death...80 years from now – are people to enter into your now-growing database.

"But", you ask, "how else am I going to grow my database from an open house?" You say, "I usually only have one to four visitors (aka leads) at my open house, that's not real database growth."

Well, let's suppose for a second that you are only growing your database by open house visitors and not yet incorporating all of the other people you can 'touch' each weekend with your open house (stay with me here, I will discuss those people in a moment).

For this example, we are going to say you do one open house per week for 40 weeks of the year (with 52 weeks in a year, that's 12 free weekends!). Your open house attendance ranges from 1-8 people for this example, so we will use 4 people per week for an average.

4 X 40 = 160

From doing the minimal amount of database growth with open houses, you are adding 160 people to your database each year! In five years, your database will grow by 800 people simply through open houses!

160 X 5 = 800

I've spoken to many agents who enter this business with a puny database or sphere of influence. I don't know about you, but to them a database of 800 is HUGE! I also speak to agents who are veterans in real estate, yet their businesses have become stale and flat. An increase of 800 people would propel their business to a new level of success. How does adding 160 people a year to your database sound to you?! Think back to where you were five years ago. Would you like to

Open House Leads by Year

4 X 40 = 160

Open House Leads in 5 Years

160 X 5 = 800

Don't rob yourself of this opportunity to grow your business!

now have 800 more people in your database than you did then?

And remember, we aren't going to stop at those 4 people per week! In later chapters I teach you how to increase your database through open house farming, FSBOs, expireds and online leads.

Neighborhood Credibility

Agents, rookie and veteran alike, come to me all the time for advice on how to dominate a neighborhood or get more listings in a particular area. They ask me about farming systems, expensive postcard systems, magazine ads and magic beans. There is a time and place for all of those legs of real estate I just mentioned (except the beans!); and when done correctly, they are part of a well-balanced real estate career. But my answer is always the same: one of the simplest and most effective ways for an agent to tap into a neighborhood is through open houses.

Imagine that you are a homeowner thinking about selling and every weekend you see Annie Agent's open house signs scattered throughout your neighborhood. Then, you turn on your computer and see Annie all over online, talking about your neighborhood and promoting her open houses. Annie is actively working your neighborhood and you take notice. When you are ready to sell, you feel compelled to call Annie for a listing appointment.

Buyers also look for the agent who is "in-the-know" to navigate them through their purchase. Align yourself through effective open houses as the neighborhood expert and you will attract more buyers – even buyer referrals from residents in your targeted neighborhood.

Between your marketing and the repeated physical presence you gain via open houses, you will establish yourself as the neighborhood expert. People will have no choice but to think of you when they think of real estate in their neighborhood! So, the next time you think open houses only exist to make your seller happy, remember

14

that the true purposes – leads, database growth and neighborhood credibility – are success-driven; they drive success to *you*.

Key Notes:

⇨Open houses are important to you because they drive leads to you, are an avenue to grow your database, and aid in increasing your neighborhood credibility.

⇨Open houses should be viewed as business-building events.

⇨Open houses provide valuable marketing exposure – for you and for listings.

⇨Buyer and seller leads come from open houses. Also, you can procure leads that don't even attend your open house.

⇨Easily grow your database by 160 people per year through open houses – that's 800 people every five years!

⇨One of your most efficient ways to gain neighborhood presence is through the use of open houses.

CHAPTER 3:

TOP 10 EXCUSES AGENTS GIVE FOR *NOT* DOING OPEN HOUSES

As I've mentioned, agents *love* to tell me all the reasons why open houses don't work for them. It starts like this: I'm standing in front of a room, beginning my class on how to strategize and market for open houses. Before I can finish my first sentence, a voice shouts out from the group, "Oh, well, *those* never work for me."

This person is brave. She's broken the silence of the group to interrupt me, the teacher. Instead of taking back control of the room, I allow the interloper to continue. She doesn't realize she is setting me up for a powerful teaching moment.

While this person drones on about why things just don't work for them, others in the room start to either agree (they've had similar failure stories) or they start to realize, "Wow, this person has a really bad attitude. I don't want to be *that* person. I better listen up so I can learn how to get good at open houses!"

What this agent is showing me, and the others in the room, is that she has a bad attitude. Her "reasons" are really excuses – excuses she's created in her mind about why she cannot be successful.

This teachable moment is all about attitude. It doesn't matter if you are at an open house, showing a client-friend a house, or paying for your groceries, a bad attitude can make any situation disastrous.

People are attracted to happiness! In real-estate-ese: potential buyers and sellers are attracted to agents who look happy and confident in the way they present themselves! If you have a bad attitude, you can almost guarantee yourself zero clients and a short-lived real estate career.

Luckily for you, readers, I know that since you are in real estate, there is a pretty high probability that you like people. Why else would you get into a business that is centered around helping people through one of their life's biggest purchases? People-people aren't characterized as having bad attitudes, so I know you have it in you to conjure up a good attitude for those open houses!

Having a bad day? Remember that a smile is like a

yawn, it can be contagious – even to yourself. So, don a big smile, even when you don't want to, and watch it stay on your face and spread to others!

Let's go back to our complainer. Perhaps she didn't start out with such a bad attitude. Her bad attitude is the result of **failing to plan for success and following through with intention**. To deal with her failure, she created excuses. Excuses will get you nowhere in this business, they will only block you from success! That's worth repeating: excuses only block you from success!

Next, I list some of the most popular excuses I hear, how you can learn from them, and advanced success tips for you to follow.

Excuse #1: "Putting signs in the ground is too hard and I hate getting out in the heat/cold/wind/rain to do it."

Putting directional signs in the ground is one of the more labor-intensive activities we have to do in this business. Sweat, mud, stained clothes, tears, dodging traffic – these are no strangers to agents when putting out signs.

Regardless, this is a crucial step for your successful open house. Directionals help visitors find your open house and they attract visitors who otherwise wouldn't have heard about your open house. They are also key components in increasing your neighborhood presence. It's a messy job, yet it's a necessary job.

Let's all take a moment to internalize that while no one likes putting out signs, it's a job that must be done. ... Got it?

Now that we have acceptance, there are some solutions to this dirty job. If you get clever, you can find *someone* to help you so you don't have to show up to your open house with sweat-stained clothes. You can hire a high-schooler looking for extra cash to put out and take down signs for you. Some handyman-type services offer this as well. Or, you can buddy up with another agent so that one of you can drive and keep the A/C going while the other jumps out to place the signs.

No one able to help? Be sure to bring an extra set of clothes with you to your open house and give yourself enough time to change and wipe down the sweat and dirt before your open house begins. Just do yourself a favor – be sure to lock the front door when changing so you don't have an unexpected early guest!

Success Tips:

⇨ Your marketing pieces are a reflection of you, including your directional signs. Make sure they look clean and professional. Clean each sign prior to your open house, so that you don't have to wipe them down as you put them into the ground.

20

⇨ Placing your directionals neatly in your car will save you from having to untangle them while you are jumping out of the car to place one on a street corner.

⇨ When using metal stakes that go into the ground, bring a jug of water with you so that you can soften ground that is too hard. If using A-frames instead, be sure to place them in grassy areas, as they are easily knocked over by wind when placed on sidewalks and roads.

Excuse #2: "You're telling me I need 10 directional signs for my open house? I can't afford that right now!"

I get it. Your previous standard for an open house was a tad lower than what is required for a successful open house. You'd show up with your glossy title company handouts, unlock a door, and sit around a stranger's kitchen table with the hope that visitors would stumble across your one open house sign. Minimal level of investment involved with this strategy.

I'm here to tell you this strategy is wrong, lethal in fact, to your business. It's time to wake up to the realization that you must invest in your business. When the owner of your favorite neighborhood restaurant opened his doors, he didn't do so without investing some serious money into his business. You should think the same way. And, while you're at it – add the restaurant owner to your open house database! (More information on beefing up your database through open houses in later chapters.)

Now you counter me and say, "But I'm not a restaurant owner for this purpose!" True, you are not a restaurant owner – but you are a *business owner*. Every agent needs to understand that they need to invest in their business, and in themselves, just like any other business owner.

In business, you need to spend money to make money. Even the six-year-old running a lemonade stand understands this concept (albeit her parents may be the ones putting up the money for the lemons and sugar). Don't have money at this time? Join a team that helps you by providing necessary materials like open house directionals.

Side story: I was out of town one weekend and had another agent hold open my listing (I prefer other agent's to hold my listings open anyway). He was eager for the opportunity and I heavily marketed the open house all week. The seller, an investor/builder, lived right around the corner from this house and he called me around what should have been half-way through the open house to tell me the agent was a no-show. I don't know who was more angry – me or the seller.

I called the agent to ask where he was. He answered, and to boil my blood further, he replied ever-so-nonchalantly, "Oh, well, I realized this morning that I only had two directionals, and I know we should always put out 10, so I just didn't show up." Can you imagine my anger levels at this point? He was **not** prepared for success!

Never flake out on a committed open house because you lack signs. On the scale of importance, commitment is at the very top and the number of directionals you use falls slightly under that. Circumvent failure and plan for success *now* – stock up on your directionals today!

To make a slightly off-topic point, I'll add the detail that my personal home was also on the market – a simple phone call to me would have provided him with instructions to access my lockbox and grab my signs from my garage (it was on his way to the open house anyway). When you get into a jam, speak up and ask for help finding a solution. You will find that other agents are happy to help you succeed in this business – and if you are not in a helping environment, it may be time to find a company with a better environment or some mentors outside of your company.

Success Tips:

⇨ Branded directional signs are worth the investment, especially since they aid in giving you repetitive neighborhood presence. If your contact info or branding is plastered all over your signs, you rule out the possibility of another agent mistakenly taking your signs home. Also, branded signs make it easier for buyers to follow your open house signs to the home – like breadcrumbs for Hansel and Gretel. And, they look more professional than the generic signs purchased at hardware stores. Buyers and sellers will notice!

⇨ To really make your signs stand out, place balloons, pinwheels or other flashy (not tacky) materials on them. I know some people are against balloons for environmental reasons, however I find them most effective. Since balloons lose their helium rather quickly, they signal that the open house is current and people don't have to worry they may be following stale directionals from last week's open house.

⇨ Feel free to go past 10 signs – the more signs you have attracting people to your open house, the more successful your open house will be! Just never fall below 10.

Excuse #3: "No one showed up to my last open house. They

don't work, so I'm not doing them anymore."

So, you had an open house where all you did was play Sudoku on your phone for three hours while no one came through the door? Have you ever shown a buyer 100 homes only to find out they took a job in another state and no longer needs to buy in your city? Have you ever lost a listing appointment to another agent? If you answered yes to either question, did you then give up on working with buyers or sellers? No, of course not (I know because you are reading this book)! Then why give up on open houses because of one bad open house experience?

You need to understand that this business is not a 1 = 1 game. One buyer doesn't represent one closing every single time. For instance, you may have 10 buyers to every 7 closings.

Real estate is a numbers game – and you must be in the game to win! The more you are out on the court playing, the more chances you have to score. I'm sure I'm messing up this sports analogy somehow, but you get the point: in order to have more closings, you need to be in front of more potential buyers and sellers. In order to be in front of more potential buyers and sellers you need to be where they are: open houses.

Ask yourself: *did I do enough marketing for my last open house? Did I have enough directionals out?* Many times you will find there is something you could have improved upon – and I will teach you those techniques you need to know so that you have a standard to hold yourself to.

Do you feel as though you did everything possible to market your open house, yet still had no traffic? Remind yourself that no two days are alike – ever. I would relentlessly hold open a listing until it sold during the housing crash a few years ago. This sometimes meant six months of open houses at a single listing. I would have weekends with zero traffic followed by a weekend where people piled into the house. There was no rhyme or reason to the date, I just had to be sure to **show up**!

> Don't let one bad open house stop you from your next open house. They are completely independent from each other.

Success Tips:

⇨ In the case of a slow open house, don't find yourself bored or playing Sudoku. Instead, be productive by writing personal letters to people in your database, writing thank you letters to previous guests, or reading a real-estate-related book.

⇨ Organize your database during slow times. Be sure to have a database system in place, such as a CRM, and that you are sending something to your database at least once a month. Nurturing your database is one of the most important "pieces of the real estate pie." If you only contact your open house leads one time after the open house, your retention rate is going to be extremely low – and in this case, open houses will be a waste of time for you. Engage your database at least once a month, whether it by an email newsletter or a coffee date – or risk losing them to another agent.

Excuse #4: "I don't have the money to do an open house the right way."

Similar to Excuse #2, this excuse is used when I urge agents to properly present themselves at an open house. After discussing how a nice spread of ice-breaking treats is an important detail, I'm met with resistance: "Oh, I can't afford to bring coffee and pastries to every open house I do. I'll go broke trying to feed all these strangers at my open houses!"

I fight my urge to roll my eyes at them. I then have them imagine two simultaneous open houses on the same street. At one of these open houses, the agent has a small but classy spread of bakery-quality pastries. Hot coffee is wafting through the air and she has a neat display of personally branded water bottles. The agent engages her visitor, a nosy neighbor, in lengthy conversation as she pours him coffee and he enjoys the treats.

Across the street is the other agent. When the same nosy neighbor walks in to this home he is not greeted by the sweet smell of cookies. Not compelled by the brochure labeled '101 Things to Do Downtown' laying next to the sign-in sheet, and with no ice-breaking treats to slow him down, he breezes past without stopping to sign in. Instead, he walks through the home and then exits after seeing all that needs to be seen. His visit felt more like a showing than an event.

Neither agent knew that the visitor disguised as a nosy neighbor was actually scouting for a listing agent that day. I ask my students, "Based on the presentation of the open houses, who do you think that seller chose to call later?" I'm sure it comes as no surprise to you that the students unanimously pick the agent who made her open house feel like an event.

Consider each open house an event – a time for you to shine and impress your visitors. Orchestrate each open house in a manner that will make an impact on your guests. Pastries and coffee will not break your bank – they are an investment into your career and can make or break the amount of leads you get from an open house.

Think about it this way – would you rather spend $50 on *cold* internet leads or $50 on making your open house look professional and stand out amongst the rest for the chance to impress *warm* leads? You'll find more success with the latter each and every time and *that* is money well-spent!

Success Tips:

⇨ Talk to your CPA about how to use your open house expenses as deductions on your annual tax return.

⇨ Don't binge on the leftover treats. Put them to good use and take them to the nearest fire or police station along with some flyers about special loan programs for public safety workers.

⇨ Find free water bottle label templates at www.ShannonEnsor.com/yktohs/resources.

Excuse #5: "I don't want to spend my weekend working."

Have you ever had this conversation with an acquaintance or someone you just met?

Them: "What do you do for a living?"

You: "I'm a real estate agent."

Them: "Oh man, that must be the best job ever! You don't have to work nine to five and can work whenever you want! I wish I had that kind of schedule!"

You: "Yeaaah. It's great! Know of anyone looking to buy or sell?"

Meanwhile, your stomach is in knots and your

inner dialogue is saying the truth, "Yeah right! All I do is work nights and weekends, AND nine to five! I have no life!"

So, when your mentor tells you to do more open houses to increase your business, you resist her. You think, "There is no way I am going to commit to *more* work during my weekend. I'm supposed to be the one with the flexible job, remember?!"

You have now created an excuse that will stunt your business. Refuse to take the necessary steps to develop and grow your business, and you'll soon have plenty of free time on your hands!

What if you are in a spot in your career where you are quite happy with your amount of closings? Let's say you have two this month and three the next. But, what about the next month? And the months after that? The moment you become complacent and stop prospecting for more business, is the moment your closings start to dry up.

The reality is that most of your prospective clients work nine-to-five jobs. This leaves them with nights and weekends for their house hunting or to be home for listing appointments. As an agent, you need to be available when the buyers and sellers are available.

Why do you think most coffee shops close as night

falls and most bars are not open in the early hours of the day? They know their target audience well, and so should you.

Remember our formula from Chapter 2? 4 X 40 = 160. There are 52 weeks in a year, so that leaves you 12 glorious weekends each year to vacation or recharge (or step up your database growth by sneaking in some extra open houses!). Set a goal to hit your 160 leads obtained from open houses and take a break. Or, you can scatter the 'free' weekends throughout the year to prevent burn out. Whatever you do, don't dismiss open houses altogether because you feel like your weekends aren't made for working. In five years, when your database is 800 people stronger because of your open house work, you'll be thankful you put in the time!

Success Tips:

⇨ In most regions, the majority of open houses are on Sunday from 1pm to 4pm, or Saturday afternoon during similar time blocks. That's when prospects know they can get in the car, drive, and happen upon some open house signs. Plan your open houses during those times when buyers expect to see open houses, and you will increase your success.

⇨ If you have a religious or familial reason for not holding a weekend open house, you do have options.

If you give all of your weekend time to your clients, you will lose precious prospecting time that takes place at open houses. Soon, you'll run out of clients.

Target a house or neighborhood near a school or busy traffic area. Then, hold the open house during the week, either right after school drop-off or right before school pick-up. This helps you target parents who have time to enjoy an open house without having to worry about corralling their kiddos. In the busy traffic areas, hold the open house during evening rush hour so people can hit up your open house while waiting for traffic to die down on their way home from work.

⇨ If you hold an open house near a school, reach out to your lender about special loan programs for public teachers and leave co-branded flyers along with your leftover coffee and doughnuts in the teachers' lounge!

⇨ Learn to time-block your schedule, as taught in Michael Maher's *7L: The Seven Levels of Communication* book, so that you can schedule 'YOU time' around work time during the weekends. Find a balance that works for you so you do not feel like you are sacrificing your free time for your business.

Excuse #6: "I want to leave my Saturday/Sunday afternoons

free for showing homes to buyers."

This can be a valid excuse if your out-of-town buyer has to see homes specifically during 1-4pm on Sunday because it's the only timeframe they have in between flights in and out of the city.

Outside that situation, it's necessary to learn how to take control of your schedule and not fear losing a client by setting time boundaries. If you give your buyer your entire weekend, they will fill it by seeing every house in the MLS because they know you have the time blocked for them. Looking at houses is usually fun for them – they don't see it as eating away at your time!

The key to making sure your weekend does not get overrun is to make a time-blocked schedule in advance. I learned this system through Maher's *7L* book and I highly recommend that you read it. It is an easy read that will change your life by teaching you how to allocate your time so you can become a more effective agent.

By time-blocking your schedule, you plan how your weekend should look ahead of time – even several weeks in advance. For example, block out 12-4:30pm each Sunday (this includes set up and take down for a 1-4pm open house). Now, you see that you have between 8am and noon available to show homes to buyers – or do a family activity or attend church. Always make sure to

33

schedule time to eat! Schedule 4:30-5-30pm for refueling yourself – and now you have 5:30-7pm to show more homes to any red-hot buyers you met at the open house, or to do a pre-listing appointment with a potential seller you just met. After 7pm can be your free time!

By planning how your Sunday should look, you can feel confident in scheduling an open house and *then* letting your clients know what times you have available for them, not the other way around.

Success Tips:

⇨ Read Michael Maher's *7L: The Seven Levels of Communication* and learn how to effectively schedule your week. You know yourself better than anyone. If you feel like doing an open house every Sunday leaves you mentally drained come Monday morning, space out your 12 free weekends. On the flip side, if you find yourself closing-poor, then schedule more open houses so you can meet more leads.

⇨ Make sure your clients have a stack of your business cards. Coach them to hand out your card and announce your representation in the case they decide to visit other open houses or model homes while you're working at your open house.

Excuse #7: "The property I'd want to hold open is in a desolate area; no one will find it." Or: *"There aren't any homes to hold open in my desired price range to work."*

I've seen many agents hem and haw over picking *just the right home* for an open house. They spend so many days deliberating on which home is best, they run out of time to market their open house properly.

I understand the logic, but it is flawed. They want to make sure they get the best bang for their buck by choosing "The Perfect House."

> Pick a home that is best for *you* – in regards to your farm – not what you think your prospects will like most.

If you are doing your marketing correctly, it should not matter which home you hold open, as long as you are holding it open with the intention of farming that area.

Take, for example, Rachel Rookie who has no listings and wants to meet new buyers through an open house. She sees that her broker has a beautiful new high-end listing, but it is far out in the country where most homes are on 10-acre sites. The home looks perfect for her open house – it is staged well and she likes that it is new to the market. However, she decides to pass because she feels as though she'd get little or no traffic because of its location and looks to see if there are any suburban homes to hold open on her office roster.

35

Rachel has yet to learn that Looky-Lous – people who are not really leads – tend to show up more to open houses in suburban neighborhoods. Perhaps it's a neighborhood they live in, or a neighborhood that is on their way to the home improvement store. It can be fun and exciting for them to visit those convenient open houses – especially if they are looking for inspiration for their next DIY project. But, the more desolate, urban areas tend to eliminate the Looky-Lous and attract more serious buyers to your open house. She wrote her broker's new listing off, not seeing the potential of meeting a strong, ready-to-go buyer.

Rachel checks out another office listing. It's a million dollar listing in one of the most prestigious neighborhoods in the city. She's intimidated. She creates two objections in her mind: 1) every buyer that comes through will probably already be signed up with Larry Luxury, the top producer in the area who specializes in luxury listings; and 2) she doubts her ability to connect with million-dollar buyers at the open house since she is so new to the industry. "They'll surely see right through me," she thinks.

In this situation Rachel's shooting herself in the foot before she even gets to the starting line of the race. Don't be like her and talk yourself out of being successful!

36

With proper practice and preparation, you will feel confident in any home you are holding open. She is also forgetting that real estate is a game of numbers. Chances are slim that *every* buyer that walks through the door will be represented by Larry Luxury – there will be some unrepresented buyers and Rachel needs to decide to show up for *them*. If she's not there, she cannot meet them.

She moves on to another listing. This home is competitively priced at $150,000 and is in a suburban community with great traffic. However, Rachel decides that while she isn't ready to tackle the luxury market, her objective is to obtain buyers in the $250,000-$400,000 range. She passes because she wants to be in a position to make a higher commission and the commission on a $150,000 home simply won't cut it for her.

Rachel has done it once again – she has passed up on the opportunity to meet tons of buyers (and sellers). You see, in this price range there is a bigger buyer pool (more people can afford this price) and many tend to be first-time homebuyers who 1) do not usually have ties to another agent like repeat homebuyers do, and 2) are scared about the home-buying process and are desperately searching for an agent to hold their hand through it all. She is ignoring a giant pool of unrepresented buyers that are eager to sign on with a buyer's representative! If she were to meet 10 buyers at the $150,000 range and make a 3% commission on all of those sales, she'd make $45,000 from that one open house – not a bad way to spend Sunday afternoon!

Instead, Rachel decides that none of these homes are "The Perfect Home", and she opts to wait for another weekend to do an open house. She gets into the habit of not doing open houses and they slowly fade out of her business model. She has cut off a leg of potential revenue and the opportunity to become a neighborhood expert. She wasn't able to win the Trivial Pursuit game because she wouldn't answer the orange question.

Rachel's decision did not affect the buyers she could have met – they found other agents at open houses. The potential sellers she missed out on meeting also found other agents – ones who had the go-getter attitude required to be a successful listing agent.

Success Tips:

⇨ Due to the declining popularity of newspapers, open house ads in print have been proven less effective. However, I have found that newspaper ads can still be effective when it comes to unique properties, such as the high-end country home on 10 acres from Rachel's example. While I won't do newspaper ads for every single open house (we agents have to invest our money wisely), I utilize them with the more obscure properties, and still find them to be quite effective.

⇨ Newspaper ads are also effective with homes that attract vacation-home buyers. Of course, those buyers use online ads just as much as anyone else, but vacationers like to grab local papers to check out the vibe of the city. This is how they learn about good restaurants and stores to visit – and open houses. Another bonus with out-of-town buyers: they are usually looking for an agent to help guide them through the city and to their next purchase. Be the agent they meet at that open house!

Excuse #8: "Everyone that comes through my open houses already has an agent."

Anyone who has this excuse on their mind needs to refer back to Excuse #3.

Remember the 'why' behind open houses. Remember that you need to be *doing* open houses to reap the benefits of open houses – which, to refresh your memory, are to attract leads, grow your database and establish neighborhood presence.

If the last 10 open house visitors already had representation agreements with other agents, isn't it possible that the next 20 will be unrepresented?! This is a numbers game and if you are not in it to win it, you are losing by default. If you never leave the bench, you can't score a homerun! (See, I do know my sports terms!)

There is nothing more important to me in real estate than NAR's Code of Ethics and I abide by them to a T. No agent should ever poach another agent's client at an open house – or in any other situation.

With that being said, if an open house visitor alerts you to the fact they are working with another agent, should you clam up and give them the cold shoulder until they exit, shredding their contact info upon departure? Absolutely not! Perhaps they will have a falling out with their agent next week. Who are they going to think of next? If you gave the cold shoulder, it certainly won't be you. But, if you were professional, cordial and showed them you have value, you will be the first agent they call!

Or, perhaps the agent they're loyal to is a family member that works in real estate part time and doesn't take any referrals outside of family. You may not get this buyer's personal business, but make a good impression and they may start sending you referrals.

In this business, the way you treat people will have rippling effects throughout your entire career. Be sure that you are professional and kind to everyone, because you never know where your next client or referral can come from!

Success Tips:

⇨ Have a space on your open house sign-in sheet for "Realtor's Name:" – this helps you quickly identify if you are speaking with a represented or unrepresented visitor. If the visitor signifies an agent and the name does not look familiar to you, look that agent up. I've seen some people write down their agent from another state. They weren't lying to me, they really had an agent – the one that is selling their out-of-state home so they can move to my city! Now you tailor your next conversation with them around becoming their local agent!

⇨ To really solidify your relationship with that lead, contact their out-of-state agent and offer them a referral fee if they can get their client to work with you exclusively in your city.

Excuse #9: "I get too nervous at open houses – I never know what to say to people when they come in."

This is a popular excuse with new and veteran agents alike. They are afraid of doing open houses – meeting people at an open house makes them feel more vulnerable and/or awkward.

Think about the general set-up of an open house: you present yourself to visitors/strangers, in the hopes they like you and want to work with you. But when you

41

hear "thanks, but no thanks", or worse, you get the condescending visitor that makes you feel like the greasiest salesman straight out of a 1970s used car lot commercial, your ego shatters. Most agents would rather play in their comfort zone with warm referrals, or field cold internet leads, than to face rejection at an open house.

I will admit, despite the millions (small exaggeration) of open houses I've done, I still get butterflies in my stomach before each one. I also get those same butterflies before a listing appointment or meeting a new buyer. This is natural. The scientific explanation includes your hypothalamus, pituitary glands and the hormone adrenaline. Simply put, it's your body's fight-or-flight mechanism. You have a work event coming up that you want to do well in, so your stress hormone adrenaline kicks in. This is your body's way of helping you make sure you are at your best by heightening your senses – or by telling you to run. I'm telling you: don't run! These little nerves help you to do well. One can even say that if you don't have butterflies, you may be approaching the situation too carelessly.

Let's say you are feeling more than little butterflies. You are straight up nervous because you feel clueless about holding an open house. You dread that a visitor will ask you a question and instead of skillfully responding, you freeze and nothing comes out of your dropped mouth but "uuuuhhh."

Although time and experience help cure this, you can pick up the pace by practicing scripts with a mentor or loved one. Be sure to pick a practice partner who understands constructive criticism is only invited when delivered with kindness. A critic who puts you down and thinks they would do better in your shoes will only make you fear open houses more. Practice with someone who shows you ways to improve and encourages you to be your best.

Preparation breeds confidence and after reading my day-by-day guide on open house preparation (the following chapters), you'll exude confidence at each of your open houses!

Even after gaining experience and mastering scripts, you need to understand something special about people. Not one person on Earth is a better person than the next. We are all equals. We were all specially created to be on this Earth for a short period of time. So, whether Donald Trump or the clerk from the 7Eleven walks into your open house, you are equally special. Confidently take every open house moment to act kindly and see if there is something you can do to help your guests with their real estate needs. Nothing more, nothing less. Simply two human beings interacting to see if they have a service to provide, an ability to purchase and the willingness to work together.

Before your open house begins and you unlock the front door so that the visitors can flood in, take three long, heavy breaths and calm your mind. Repeat to yourself that each person that walks in the door is just as special as you, and you have a service to offer them that can be the very best experience they've ever had.

Success Tips:

⇨ Have another agent or spouse or friend sit at the open house with you. Not only will they help calm your nerves, but they add a level of security. (Sadly, there are people in this world who target solo open house agents. And, I've even heard of a story where two agents were attacked at an open house. However, two agents can intimidate an attacker slightly more than a solo agent in most cases.) If you have another agent sit with you, work out a system of how leads will be handled *before* the open house as to avoid any conflict later down the road.

⇨ Take it a step further and have a loan officer join you at your open house. This way, buyers who have not yet been qualified can get started on the spot. It's a wonderful way to add value to your potential clients. The loan officer can also help answer any tricky financial questions that you may not know the answer to and they give you an extra bump in confidence. Find a loan officer that matches your personality style and that has a proven track record. Also, choose one that will help give you credibility in front of the customer. For example, the loan officer mentions to the customer, "Oh, you are lucky to get to work with Jim here, he is one of the best agents in the area!" This third-party credibility can go a long way.

⇨ If someone stumps you at your open house with a question, don't make up an answer. Instead, make sure you have their correct contact information so that you can speak with your broker and follow up with them later. Trust me, they will not see this as a sign of weakness and instead will appreciate that you take extra care in providing them with accurate information. And now you have a reason to reach out to them after the open house and continue to build rapport with them!

Excuse #10: "No one ever buys the house at an open house."
As the seller makes their house sparkle and shine Sunday morning and they trek out the door with family in tow, filling their afternoon with activities so they can stay away from the home, their every thought is imagining the near-moment when their agent calls to say, "Meet me at

the office! We received an offer from the open house!" In some markets, they are hoping to hear, "We received multiple offers today from the open house!"

However, we agents know that this is rarely the case. We know that the open house gives the home good exposure and the right buyer may be found at the open house, but it doesn't happen every single time.

While the open house visitors that pass on making offers are no longer useful to the sellers, they are certainly of great use to you, the agent!

When I hear Excuse #10, I wonder if the agent really only cares about getting one lead from the open house – the *one* who wants to buy *that* house. Agents, please do not be shortsighted – realize the bigger picture with your open houses. Each person that walks through the door can be your next buyer, seller or referral source. The amount of closings that come from an open house are limitless, reaching far past the address you hold open.

I want you to look further than the people that walk through your open house door and beyond their referrals. I want you to look around the neighborhood in which you are focusing your open houses and see all neighbors, all FSBOs, local business owners, and even expired listings as your audience. That's right, you are taking your open houses to a whole new level that gives you exposure in the area you want to farm – this is a HUGE concept for creating more growth in your business!

Now do I have your attention? It should be very clear to you that open houses are your key to dominating a neighborhood and meeting a limitless supply of potential clients – not for the purpose of selling just one home.

Success Tips:

⇨ Always be prepared for success! If a visitor says, "I love it! Where do I sign?" – jump on their momentum and have a contract ready for them to sign. Be sure to have all necessary addendums and disclosures ready to go so that you can hand over a complete offer package to the listing agent.

⇨ If your open house is teeming with visitors, you won't want to ignore the rest of your potential clients by going over the contract package with the hot buyer. Confidently make an appointment at your office or back at the house after the open house to write the contract. If the buyer sees value in you and understands that you are ready to go with the contract as soon as the open house is over, they will respect your time management skills and meet back with you.

⇨ Take it a step further, have gift cards to a local coffee shop handy; give that red-hot buyer a gift card and tell them to enjoy while you wrap up the open house. This will emotionally tie them to you, and you won't have to worry about them flaking out in the meantime.

Key Notes:

⇨Successful people are never characterized by bad attitudes and they don't allow excuses to impede their goals!

⇨Potential clients are attracted to happy, confident agents.

⇨Don't let labor-intensive activities prevent you from success. Either accept them or find someone to help.

⇨Invest in your career – this includes open house material so that you look professional at each open house and can reach the highest amount of leads possible.

⇨Each open house is independent from the last. Don't let past failure prevent you from staying in the game.

⇨Be where the leads are. Invest your time so that you reap the rewards.

⇨Be intentional with your location and the house will not matter as much.

⇨Preparation breeds confidence.

⇨The open house is not your end-game, but a stepping stone to more business.

CHAPTER 4:

MECHANICS OF A SUCCESSFUL OPEN HOUSE

Now that you understand the important role open houses play in building your real estate career and we have overcome the most common objections to open houses, you are ready to take action! There are two important mechanics behind an open house. One hinges on the location of your open house – are you properly strategizing so your efforts give you the most success? The other depends on turning your open house guests into clients – which is accomplished through rapport building. Get these mechanics in motion and you will have a successful career built on open houses!

Location, Location, Location

The first thing you will want to do is identify an area that you would like to farm or would like to work in most. Whether you want to be a niche-agent or you are happy working all four cardinal points of your city, there is that *one* area you can identify that you'd really like to target. Many agents pick the area they live in, since their daily presence in this area is advantageously high. Some pick a neighborhood they wished they lived in or the hottest area at the moment. Whatever area you pick, prepare to OWN it!

I began my career by doing open houses wherever the wind would blow me. You had a house, I would hold it open! My initial efforts were spread too thin, and I was unable to capitalize on the benefits an agent receives when they hold repetitive open houses in a single area.

Let me illustrate. I live in Austin, TX. As a new agent I'd typically do two open houses a weekend – one on Saturday, one on Sunday. In the course of a month, I'd have eight *different* open houses: from Round Rock to South Austin, then from Manor to West Austin, then from downtown to Cedar Park, then from central Austin to Dripping Springs! I was grabbing at what I could and showing up to the game, but I was not making my presence memorable in any given area.

During my haphazard open house spree, I chose an office listing in a subdivision in Manor (a city east of

Austin): ShadowGlen. I had helped a buyer in ShadowGlen in the prior year, so I was already familiar with the neighborhood – which was a 45-minute drive from my south Austin condo. At that open house I met a sweet couple who lived in the same neighborhood and they asked me to come over after my open house to talk about selling their home. I listed their home, and then began holding their house open every weekend until it sold.

In true snowball effect, from those open houses came more ShadowGlen buyers and more sellers. I even established a great working relationship with the builder's on-site salesperson (they were still building in this community) and he began to give me business. I spent every weekend in Manor, in a city/community that I never imagined farming or developing a strong base of business in; but because of the momentum of one open house, I had a steady stream of business flowing in.

People would come up to me at open houses or send me emails saying, "I see you all over the place in ShadowGlen! You are one busy girl! Tell me how values are doing in the neighborhood. Do you think it is a good time for me to sell?"

Because of my repetitive weekend presence, I was perceived as one of the neighborhood's top agents, even from people I hadn't formerly met. My neighborhood credibility had skyrocketed!

Do you see how easily you can apply this strategy to an area you would like to work and soon be thought of as the area specialist? When you use the repetitive nature of open houses to your advantage, people will notice and you will become associated with that neighborhood in their minds.

Rapport-Building Strategies

If you are a new agent, or an agent that hasn't broken into the listing side of things yet, you naturally have to ask another agent for permission to hold their listing open (my preferred method of holding an open house). More on that in a bit. I'd first like to have a small discussion on the topic of choosing your own listing as your open house.

Proponents of holding your listing open are:

1) Your listing is in a neighborhood you are farming, so it seems like a natural pick.
2) You think your seller will only allow you to hold it open.
3) You earned the listing so you want to be the one to get all possible leads from the listing.

I'm going to counter those points for you because

you deserve to think bigger in your business than they allow. Spread your visibility past your single listing in a neighborhood and hold a different listing open. It's wonderful if you have multiple listings in your targeted neighborhood – I still want you to think wider and hold other agents' listings open.

Have a controlling seller that prefers you to do all the showings and open houses? Inform them that you will properly educate the open house agent on the home's details. Let them know that the open house agent is held to the same fiduciaries as every other agent in your brokerage; and the agent follows the same safety standards as other showing agents.

Do not worry about losing leads from your listing's open house - you will grab the same leads from the other open house you are doing down the street that isn't your listing! As long as you are still showing up in your neighborhood, your neighborhood presence isn't suffering by not holding *your* listing open.

Perhaps you have the only office listing in your desired area and your broker prohibits holding open other brokerages' listings. In this scenario, I advise you to team up with another agent in your office and co-host the open house at your listing.

Why am I making these arguments against holding

open your own listing? Simple: you build stronger rapport at open houses when you are not the listing agent.

I can see your puzzled looks now, so let's imagine an open house that you're hosting for your listing. The first couple walks in. They tour the home and meet you back at the kitchen table. You ask them how they like the house. They can tell it is your listing since your name tag matches the sign in the yard, so they respond in one of these ways to your question:

1) They clam up – they know you're a salesman representing the other side so they hold their cards tight to their chest and don't give away any details. They quickly leave and decide to visit a few more open houses before making a decision.

2) They did not like the house and begin telling you all the reasons why, "Rooms are too small, price is too high, fixtures are outdated." You have two moves – a) defend the home and completely offend the visitors who were merely offering up their opinion, or b) you start to tell them about the bigger, nicer house down the street that is priced way better. Yikes! As you can see, you have no right move here – you

either turn the buyers off or you sound disloyal to your listing, neither of which builds trust with these homebuyers.

3) They love the house, it is all they've ever dreamed of and they are ready to sign on the dotted line! Now you have to pump the brakes, inform them that you cannot perform as a dual agent and that everything they say can and will be held against them when you go back to your seller. You could learn they want to waive representation or they ask you to refer them to an agent (a referral fee is a nice bonus!); but more commonly they will be frightened, as they have just said too much to the opponent. To quote Dr. Evil in *Austin Powers*, "It got weird, didn't it?"

> It is better to hold open a listing that is not your own, since you will have a higher success rate with building trust and starting a relationship with those customers – which is exactly the goal of your open house.

Maybe you consider yourself a smooth agent who can diffuse the situations above. I know I could and that I have. I've held countless open houses at my own listings. Did I build rapport at those open houses? Certainly. But I have also witnessed firsthand that rapport is easier to build with customers when I am not the listing agent. I want you to learn from my trials and errors so that you can have optimal success!

If you insist on holding your listing open, keep the following key points in mind. First, give full disclosure to your visitors so that you don't fall into the trap of falsely representing yourself. They may hold their cards tighter, but they will appreciate your integrity, which speaks louder in terms of rapport building.

Also, have an agent in mind whom you can refer any contract-ready buyers to – that way you can control at least getting a referral fee instead of leaving the buyers on their own to find an agent.

Lastly, remember that not everyone that walks through the door will want to buy your listing. Be prepared to switch into 'buyer agent mode' when they have ruled out the property – but be sure not to bad-mouth your own listing. Instead, gently acknowledge their needs aren't met with this house and shift gears to determine what will fit their needs. Maintaining a good attitude about your listing will signal to the potential clients that you would hold the same integrity for their home if they hired you to sell it.

I once had an agent tell me she thought she lacked credibility if she wasn't the listing agent at the open house (she also had very little listing experience). Her perception of low credibility was something she created in her mind – an excuse stopping her from succeeding! Do not let these excuses creep in and stop you from success. If the open house guest expects you to be the listing agent when you are not, you have several cards in your pocket to use to your advantage:

⇨ You have a working relationship with the listing agent and because of your excellent skills, they have entrusted you to be their go-to open house agent. Now you have built third-party credibility – another agent says you are a good agent.

⇨ The listing agent switches with you and you hold each other's listings open, as you both work the area and consider each other trusted agents to get a job done well. Again, this builds third-party credibility and signals that you are part of a system can serve their needs well.

⇨ The listing agent refuses to hold their house open because they realize they cannot represent the buyers that walk through the door. This gives them a greater understanding of how representation works and shows that you are welcomed by the listing agent to be their buyers' agent.

⇨ Even though you don't personally have a listing, you work closely with other agents in your office who help you and bring experience and credibility to you. (If you don't have experience, be sure that you are in an office where you can build on others' experience and have a mentorship so that buyers and sellers alike understand they are in good hands.) Take the burden of inexperience off your shoulders and rely on others to help bring you up through the ranks.

Take these tidbits and use them to your advantage – don't let the lack of listings or experience stop you from growing your business – it'll never get off the ground if you do!

You've already learned by now that holding someone else's listing open is the ideal open house situation – let's dive into the reason why. I have found that this is my #1 icebreaker when people come into the open house. After introductions, I tell visitors, "In a bit I'll ask you for feedback, and I want you to feel that you can be completely honest with me. I'm not the listing agent, so there's no way you can offend me." In this moment I see a look of relief sweep over their faces. Their guards are let down. And now, they have an important role – to unleash all their thoughts on the home à la HGTV. Boy do people love to feel like they are on their personal episode of

House Hunters! They can't wait to share with you all their thoughts on the home – enabling you to listen to their needs and learn how you can help them. The more they open up to you, the more opportunities you have to go on to further develop your relationship with them. This is rapport-building at its finest!

Did you see what else is at work when I asked them to share their thoughts with *me*? I'm creating a bond between the two of us. When you tell someone their thoughts and opinions are important to you, you are automatically moved up a few notches in their 'people I like' column. Create a bond with your words, let people know they matter, and you will effortlessly build rapport with your guests.

Once you have rapport, you can move into the next step, which is becoming their agent and selling a house!

Thoughts on Time

Another popular question I am asked is, "When is the best *time* to hold an open house?" A hopeful look follows the question, as if I'm about to whip out my magic ball and reveal the winning secret date and time formula.

Agents, remember: you have to be in it to win it, so as long as you are *doing* open houses (and let's say it's not at an unreasonable time like 2am!), you are on the right

59

path.

In my region, Sundays from 1pm to 4pm and then Saturdays from noon to 3pm tend to be the most popular times. I tend to favor open houses on Sunday over Saturday because that is the unspoken official open house day – meaning that is when house hunters assume the most open houses will be occurring – and you want to be there when the most hunters gather, don't you?! Of course, if things are slightly different in your region, follow those norms. And, keep in mind the value of a mid-week open house.

In the following chapters, you are going to get a day-by-day game plan for your weekend open house. Most items can be done in the same order in the timeline regardless if your open house is Saturday or Sunday. Shift the timeline accordingly if you are doing a mid-week open house.

Key Notes:

⇨Step 1: Chose your location with intention.

⇨Step 2: Build rapport with everyone you meet through your open house.

⇨You have stronger diversification and rapport-building when you hold another agent's listing open.

CHAPTER 5:

DAY #1 - TUESDAY

We begin our open house planning on Tuesday. Other than the day of your open house, Tuesday is your most labor intensive day. You will want to time-block a significant portion of your Tuesdays for open house preparation.

Oh, wait. You thought an open house just required three to four hours of your time on Sunday? If so, I must say you are sadly underprepared for success, my friend. If you are not putting in the preparation time for your open house, you are going to come up short at every open house – less leads, less database growth and less neighborhood dominance. Are you okay with only receiving a little reward for your efforts on Sunday? I didn't think so! You are in it to win it and are here to make open houses a well-oiled system in your real estate wheelhouse! For massive rewards, you will need to put in the preparation time – and this time starts on Tuesday.

First, select your open house. Go to your office roster and select the community/communities that are in your chosen focus area (remember, we're focusing on holding other agents' listings).

If there is not an available listing in your specific community, define adjoining communities or ones that attract move-up or move-down buyers either to or from your area. What other communities compete for buyers with your subject community? These are all excellent targets for your open house and for growing your presence in your desired area.

Take a look at those homes on the roster and contact listing agents to ask permission to hold an open house. Send a mass email or text so that they understand you are contacting more than one agent and they need to be prompt with their response. When leaving voicemail, make sure this is also implied so that you are not overpromising open houses to multiple agents.

Strategies for picking your home include:

⇨ Begin with the houses that have the least days on market (DOM) and work your way up.

⇨ Begin with homes that are vacant yet staged, for ease of open house set up. At the very least, you want to be sure the house you are holding is nicely staged. This profession is all about first impressions, and if you are meeting buyers and sellers at 'ugly' open houses, they will think you don't take the time to properly market your homes (even if the listing is not yours).

⇨ Target homes with good traffic flow first – ones tucked away in the back of a community can be your runners-up (but, remember, those can be great open houses, too!).

⇨ Target homes where nearby open houses are being planned – people tend to flock to larger scale open house events.

Once you have your subject property locked down, be sure that the listing agent is completing all the necessary tasks on their end. The listing agent's duties include contacting the owners for permission/letting them know to be out of the home, and placing the open house in the MLS system and the other syndication methods that only listing agents have access to (Zillow/Trulia, for example). Stay on top of the agent to make sure these tasks are taken care of. Also, realize that each listing agent will vary when it comes to the amount of advertising they do on their end. If you get an agent that spends money on Facebook marketing, then great! But don't expect or harass them to do so – you will have your marketing in place regardless of their efforts.

Next, contact your favorite lender and get them started on creating your financial flyers for the open house. This is a valuable piece for you to hand out to prospective buyers, as it outlines different loan programs and monthly payments if they were to buy the house. It's also your gateway to having the "have you spoken to a lender yet?" talk and to learn more about their house-buying needs ("Oh, from these loan scenarios you see that a house in the $X price range would get you into your monthly payment comfort-zone. Are you available tomorrow or Tuesday to take a look at some of the homes that meet your criteria?").

Success tip: ask your lender to sit with you at the open house. In addition to bringing the flyers, lenders will most likely share in the open house costs with you. Their knowledge and ability to pre-qualify on the spot adds value to your visitors, boosting your credibility. Be sure to choose a lender who matches or complements your sales style so that you can smoothly bounce conversation off of each other with the buyer.

Thorough Planning = Database Building

Now your legwork really begins. Go to Google Maps (or whichever map program you prefer) and determine all entry points into the neighborhood and the roads leading to those points. Place stars on all the places where you should put your directionals. Later, when you visit the community, you will select more points of interest that lead to your open house – for example, signs leading from community parks to your open house. You want to clearly and effectively route the most amount of traffic to your open house. Your ultimate aim is to have at least 10 directionals. (Note: you are *not* putting your directionals out today – those should go out just before your open house.)

From looking at the map, determine how many signs will be in someone's yard. Prepare notes to place on their doors, asking permission for your signs to be in their yards during your open house. These notes should be written on your personal letterhead and say:

"Hello! I'm holding an open house for your neighbor at (address) on Sunday, (date) from (start/end time). We'd really appreciate it if we could place a sign in your yard during the open house. I will be sure to pick it up promptly after the open house and will respect your yard as I place it in the ground. Please contact me if this will be a problem for you. I'll have refreshments at the open house and would love it if you stopped by! And, if you know of anyone who'd like to move to (neighborhood name), please invite them!"

Sign your name and enclose a business card. Have a template saved on your computer to save time each Tuesday. This note is powerful and you'll see why in a moment.

I'll never forget, about halfway through one of my first open houses, I received an angry phone call from a neighbor whose yard I had used for my directional sign. (He got my number off of my branded directional sign, of course!) Up to this point, I had done a couple of open houses where I had taken the liberty of placing signs in yards with no thought to asking permission. I thought this was the norm – no one had taught me differently. Well, from the tone of his voice and the language he used, I sure did learn I was wrong! I immediately apologized and told him I'd be over promptly to get my sign. He must've felt bad for shaking me up, because he allowed me to come after the open house – but only if I promised to come ring his doorbell. After the open house, I gathered the remainder of my freshly-baked chocolate chip cookies and humbly marched to his house.

Nervous, I rang the doorbell and held out the cookies. Luckily sweet treats are superb peace offerings and he did not continue to berate me for "assuming I could use his yard as my marketing tool." It turns out, I was about the fifth agent to hold his neighbor's house open, and not one of us had thought to ask permission to use his prime corner spot. He had hit his limit with agents using his yard, and I had taken the brunt of his frustration earlier over the phone. I learned that day to never, *not ever*, put a sign in someone's yard without their permission.

Tip: Bring plastic wrap and decorative paper plates to your open houses so that you can pack up your leftover treats for easy distribution!

This is why your next step on the Tuesday-before-an-open-house is to visit the homes that are key locations for your signs on Sunday, and ring the doorbell in hopes to ask the residents for permission. Note that this is a great way to talk to the neighbors and introduce them to your professional, kind face – which means this is impression time, so look the part!

When they open their door, *nicely* ask for permission to place a sign in their yard during the open house. Be sure to invite them to your open house and **ask if they know of anyone looking to move into their neighborhood that you could also invite**. Do you see what you are doing with this step? You are creating a referral path with this person. Even if they cannot think of someone today, they will think of you the next time they hear of someone wanting to move to their area! Be sure to leave two business cards with them – or better yet, your marketing brochure.

If you don't get an answer, leave your note on their door. (Aren't you glad that you took the time to write the notes *before* venturing into the neighborhood?! Utilize time-saving strategies every chance you get.)

You've now potentially met eight to ten neighbors and introduced yourself as the neighborhood agent. ADD THEM TO YOUR DATABASE. If you were given a referral, ADD THEM TO YOUR DATABASE. For the neighbors that weren't home, you left a professional note on their door with your branding, ADD THEM TO YOUR DATABASE. You have five days before your open house and your database, and guest list, is already growing!

In addition, these neighbors have now been introduced to your name and branding, something that is about to be in their face repeatedly via your open house signs and other marketing material that we will discuss in a bit. Through this repetition, you are developing yourself as the neighborhood expert who will come to their minds when they have real estate needs.

Day #1 - Tuesday

Preparation Builds Confidence – and Leads

Next, you want to visit the home you are holding open, with advance seller permission of course. The seller will be happy that you are doing your homework so that you can properly represent their home at the open house, so this is a welcomed call.

As the listing agent, I like to meet my open house agent at this preview so that I can highlight all the features of the home and prepare them on how to best show off the house on Sunday.

Another important tip for listing agents: be sure to coach your sellers to not blab to the open house agent about their situation, e.g., how desperate they are to sell. Your seller understands that you work in the same office, so they will feel a level of trust with the open house agent. But if they spill the beans that they "want to be moved out *yesterday* and will take any low-ball offer," you can guarantee that the open house agent will share that detail with a buyer they find at the open house!

Take notes and pictures as you tour the home. Also, be sure to place an "Open Sunday" rider in the sign, or a sign in the yard that tells the date and time of the open house. This helps you gather more interested buyers – **leads** – throughout the week, which is why it is crucial to get the sign out as soon as you know you'll be holding the open house.

Next, drive the neighborhood once more. Find area amenities such as community centers, pools and playgrounds. Jump out of your car and take pictures of the amenities and of anything else of interest in the neighborhood. No amenities? Find walking paths, or nearby schools and businesses. I'll tell you why in a moment.

Database Building with FSBOs and Expireds

Open houses are a powerful leg of your business because they bleed into other areas – such as developing FSBO and expired sellers. Most times, FSBOs and expireds are equated to cold calls. With proper implementation, you can create a warm approach to these two types of sellers, increasing your success ratios.

While you are still scouting your open house neighborhood, locate any FSBOs in the neighborhood. Stop at those homes and speak with the sellers. Let them know that you are holding their neighbor's house open and, if they are willing to cooperate with a buyer's agent, you'd like to get details on their home. Explain that this helps you determine if their home is a better match for prospective buyers whose needs aren't met with your subject home.

See if they'll take you on a tour of their home. You are now building rapport with this FSBO, and they'll be more likely to work with you if you have a buyer. Also, you will sound more knowledgeable to your open house visitors who ask about "the FSBO down the street." And, if the FSBO gives up on FSBOing, guess who'll be on their mind to call to list their home?! Be sure to right down the address of all FSBO's in the neighborhood and ADD THEM TO YOUR DATABASE!

Next, pull out your mobile MLS app and see if there are any expireds in the neighborhood. (Expireds are homes that have recently fallen off the market and are no longer represented by an agent). With the same helpful mindset that you approached the FSBOs with, speak with these homeowners and learn if they are still interested in selling. Explain that if you run into a buyer at the open house that has been dutifully scouting the neighborhood for months, they are going to ask what happened to the listing that used to have the for sale sign in the yard – and you'd like to sound informed when they ask. Whereas every other agent has contacted the expired seller to get their listing, you are reaching out for help – you're asking them to help you sound informed at your open house. You now have a warm introduction.

This leads you to the question, "If I found a buyer,

would you still be interested in selling?" If you find them a buyer at your open house, fantastic! If you don't find a buyer for them from your open house, that's okay, too – you have now ADDED THEM TO YOUR DATABASE and have a better foot in the door than any other agent in town!

When I discuss adding FSBOs and expireds to your database, I mean for you to have a game plan in place for nurturing these leads. Follow up your conversations with handwritten thank you cards. Add them to your newsletters and farming postcards. Send them market reports. And, most importantly, send them your marketing information so they learn that you are not just a buyer's agent – you also have a system in place to *sell* their home!

When they see you doing open houses in their neighborhood, weekend after weekend, they'll recognize you as the neighborhood expert. Your open houses will pave the way for domination of all the FSBOs and expireds in your targeted area!

Marketing Exposure, Leads and Neighborhood Dominance – The Blogging & Social Media Trifecta

You've explored the neighborhood and talked to a handful of the neighbors. Now, it's time to go home and start marketing.

If you don't have a personal website, I recommend that you get one, as it is another important leg of your real estate career. If you work at a team or office that has substantial online presence and allows you to blog on their site, this works, too.

Take your notes and pictures and turn them into a blog about the neighborhood. Even the tiniest of neighborhoods or sub-neighborhoods are good subjects when it comes to blogging.

If this is your first time blogging about the neighborhood, leave out the information about the open house. You will use the blog in your open house marketing, but you want longevity with this flagship neighborhood blog on your site, so leave out the open house details this time. As you do sequential open houses in the neighborhood, you will create them about the open house and any neighborhood updates. Make sure you link to your original neighborhood blog in your sequential open house blogs.

Structure:

First Neighborhood OH:	"These are all the reasons why this neighborhood is so great...."
Sequential OHs for that Neighborhood:	"Remember that neighborhood I told you about before (first blog link)? Here's what's been going on in it, plus another chance to check it out at my open house this weekend!

If the word "blog" intimidates you, relax! There is no perfect blog. Simply give your personal account of what you thought about the neighborhood during your tour. A blog should have your personality shining throughout it – I suggest writing as if you were telling a friend about the neighborhood. You want the readers to connect to *you*. This connection allows your name to pop in their minds later when they think of the neighborhood.

Avoid negativity in your blog! Think of yourself as the self-appointed public relations person for this neighborhood. While you cannot lie, you do not need to highlight anything negative (for example, if the community pool has not been well-kept, leave out the part about it being green and just mention that there is a community pool).

Also, avoid sounding like an encyclopedia entry for

the neighborhood – give it life! Rather than stating: "This community has two parks and is by the elementary school," say: "As I turned onto the tree-lined streets of the community, I was drawn to the shaded park where families were playing after school."

As a general blogging rule, keep your sentences and paragraphs short and add your pictures for visual effect and better SEO (search engine optimization) properties. Don't overthink this blog! Give yourself thirty minutes to an hour to write it and move on!

The most important element of your blog is your call to action. Let readers know that you are the neighborhood expert (you spent all day getting to know it, I believe you've earned this title!) and that you are the agent to call for their real estate needs. Allow comments and make sure you have a lead capture system that asks visitors if they'd like to sign in to view MLS listings, or even submit their email for your monthly newsletter and blog updates. Follow these steps and your blog will turn into a source of **leads** for you, even long after your open house.

When you post your blog, you have two more things happening for you. For one, you are creating a tool to point to when you invite people to your open house and for use in your advertising. And two, your blog is now on the internet for all to see for as long as you leave it up (forever hopefully!). Now, when people do a web search about the neighborhood, your blog will be something they see. You become the neighborhood expert in their eyes. You are also creating neighborhood credibility when prospective clients go online to research you – and you can bet that almost all of your clients will go online to research you!

Important note: Never plagiarize words or use other people's pictures in your blog – not only is this illegal and lazy, you will only be hurting yourself. Duplicate content is punished by online search engines – if your blog is not original, you will not rank in the searches. If you are creating a neighborhood blog for your personal website and your company's website, the same rules apply – make each blog unique from each other. Search engines even read picture pixels. So when taking neighborhood photos, snap one and then move a foot to your left and snap another from a slightly different angle, then use them on separate blogs.

I'm going to make another assumption of you as an agent – that not only do you have a website or access to one, but that you are utilizing social media to help boost your real estate career. Whether it is Facebook (my personal favorite) or Twitter or LinkedIn, I am hoping that you have already established a presence. If not, it is time!

Go to your social media accounts and post a link to your blog. In that post, invite everyone and their mothers to your open house! I know, it's only Tuesday – but the goal isn't for people to mark your open house on their calendars, it is to link to your blog and direct people to go to your blog. This gives your blog traction and will help it in the search engine ranks. Rank well in the search engines and you will receive more leads when people go online to research a community. When people see your blogs, they will assume you are a neighborhood expert!

Circling back to inviting people to the open house, if you are a Facebooker, spend some money to boost your open house/blog link post. I tend to spend about $20 on Facebook ads per open house. Adjust to what is suitable for your budget. Be sure to boost it through the end date of your open house, in order to get maximum exposure. If you boost past the open house, you may confuse your audience (unless you are solely boosting the neighborhood blog without open house information).

To recap how you have made this a very successful Tuesday, you've met neighbors, FSBOs and expireds; resulting in database growth, an increase in neighborhood presence, and potential lead sources. You have posted a blog and began marketing your open house online –

increasing your credibility as a neighborhood expert and creating a new avenue for leads. You are now familiar with the neighborhood and the home, which means you are more confidently prepared for a successful open house on Sunday.

The Farming Connection

Before we move on to Thursday (that's right, you get Wednesday for your other pie pieces!), I am going to suggest one more step: farming letters. You know your budget best – and I do hope that you've sat down, and on top of writing your goals, you have devised your real estate marketing budget. Even if your budget shifts each time you have a closing (I should say grows rather than shifts!), continually take the time monitor your budget and prevent over- or under-spending.

Keep in mind, you are holding open houses in an area or neighborhood that you want to work and that you see value in farming. Farming is another piece of your real estate pie. And, it just so happens that your open house efforts will play nicely into your farming. In fact, when you send pieces of information to your farm about the open houses you are doing, you are sending them a message that you are actively working their neighborhood – much more effective than a postcard with a pie recipe!

For this step, you're going to need to budget ideally $100 for each open house mail-out. You will print an open house invite to 200 of the surrounding neighbors (who are a part of your farm) and mail them on Tuesday. (200 stamps at the current rate of $0.49 = $98.) I find 200 homes to be an effective number, however, play around with these numbers to fit your budget best. For example, if $50 is your current budget, then you will only be targeting 100 houses with your mail-out, and so forth.

Compile the list of addresses from your board's tax system (we use Realist in Austin). I only mail to the addresses physically in the neighborhood, not to out-of-town homeowners/investors, so that I contact the renters that live in the neighborhood who may be "trying before buying." If you are savvy with the tax system's search features, you will want to get the most out of your 200 addresses by choosing people who have owned their home for at least three years, this way you target people who are more apt to want to sell soon.

If you are going to do this step, you need to commit to getting your letters out on Tuesday so they can hit mailboxes in time for your open house. Luckily, you are going to have a system in place so that this will not be a time-consuming step.

Your letter should be printed on your letterhead

and look something like this (pardon the style break, an example can be found at www.ShannonEnsor.com/yktohs/resources):

You're Invited!

Another Great Open House

by Shannon Ensor!

123 Elm Street

Elmwood Subdivision

Sunday February 30th

1-4pm

Please stop by for some refreshments and valuable information for Elmwood homeowners!

Know anyone who'd like to live in your neighborhood?

Invite them, too!

There will be a drawing for a

$50 gift card to Elmwood Steakhouse!

Recent Market Activity for Elmwood

Property Type: Residential				Status: Sold				Number of Properties: 6		
	Beds	Baths	SqFt	Listing Price	LP/SqFt	Selling Price	SP/SqFt	SP/LP	SP/OLP	DOM
High	5	4	2,879	$474,000	$214.07	$467,000	$213.57	99.8%	98.5%	52
Low	4	2	2,004	$369,900	$145.88	$347,500	$140.12	88%	88%	6
Average	4	3	2,366	$417,717	$179.09	$404,333	$173.63	96.68%	96.45%	22
Median	4	2	2,372	$419,250	$177.5	$411,250	$174.14	98.1%	98.05%	16

Last 3 months of solds for single-family homes in Elmwood.

Need help selling your home? Let's talk about it!

Contact Shannon Ensor today!

555-555-5555 or shannonsellselmwood.com

You can play around with this letter to suit you, but here is a breakdown of the key components.

⇨ You're personally inviting them to your open house – this takes away the awkwardness of the nosy neighbor. This letter alone has changed nosy neighbors from dodging me as soon as they come in the door to introducing themselves and saying, "I'm here because I received your letter." There's warmth to the situation now – you want them to be there and they came.

⇨ "Another Great Open House" – this shows them you're an active agent in the area. Fake it 'til you make it if you have to! They don't have to know if it's your first – you've said "another", so it must be true. Color them impressed by you!

⇨ "Please stop by for refreshments and valuable information..." – again, you are inviting them to be there. As a bonus, they'll be rewarded with refreshments. More importantly, now you've piqued their interest. They wonder, "What is this valuable information?" The answer: more neighborhood market stats and inventory report that you'll prepare on Saturday, a market outlook (think overall stats and information about your area/city such as job growth and interest rates), and a brochure with tips for preparing a house for sale. Those last two are items that you can keep in your running inventory, creating less work for you on Saturday; we'll go over these in more depth when we hit Saturday's chapter.

⇨ Asking them to invite their friends and family – increases your odds of a great buyer coming your way. It is quite common for people to tell their loved ones to keep an eye out for homes for sale in their neighborhood. By asking them to invite others, you are telling these residents, "Hey, I can be your friend's agent, too! I love referrals!"

⇨ $50 gift card – everyone loves free stuff! I encourage you to make the gift card to something local and popular as opposed to generic coffee shop or store. Why? Because people love "local" – make the connection in their minds that you are a part of that local vibe.

⇨ Market stats – if someone plans to come to your open house, they'll keep your letter hanging around their house for a few days, giving more chances for your name and branding to stick in their mind. What if they don't plan to come? Prevent your letter from going straight into the garbage by giving them value in this letter! Whether people are planning to sell soon or not for another 10 years, everyone likes to stay abreast of what is going on with their home values. Market stats are something they'll appreciate – you've given them a piece of value – and they solidify you as a neighborhood expert.

⇨ "Need help selling your home?" – your last call-to-action. As an agent, you *must* have a call to action in every piece of marketing. Show them that you have the confidence to talk about listing their home – whether or not they make it to the open house, tell them *you* are the agent to call for their real estate needs.

As you can see, this letter is a powerful open house. And, what do you do next with these 200 homes that you're mailing letters to? That's right – you ADD THEM TO YOUR DATABASE! This is why it is so important to target a specific neighborhood or area. If you are doing your open houses in a similar area each weekend, then when you mail out your 200 letters each week, you are going to have overlaps of people getting 1 – 4 pieces of mail from you each month....or 10 – 40 a year! If you are already a fan of farming, I bet your head is spinning with excitement from these numbers!

Furthermore, I want you to really manage these databases. Pay attention to when the house you held open sells and mail another letter to the people who received your open house letter: *"My firm sold 123 Elm Street, ask me how our proven marketing systems can sell your home, too!"*

Whatever you do, don't send one letter to these people and forget about them. Repetition is key when it comes to farming. Cultivate your open house/farming database and you will become the go-to neighborhood expert in that area!

If you are fretting right now because you are a new agent who cannot afford to send out these letters each week, don't worry, I have a solution for you on Day #2!

Key Notes:

⇨Schedule your weekend open house on Tuesday to gain maximum marketing exposure.

⇨No houses available in your farm? Choose homes in adjoining or move-up/move-down communities.

⇨Partner with a trusted lender for marketing material.

⇨Identify where you will place your directionals on Tuesday, making sure to ask for neighbor permission.

⇨Tour the community and home prior to the open house.

⇨Grow your database through FSBOs and expireds.

⇨Blogging and social media will increase your leads and neighborhood credibility.

⇨Increase seller leads through open house invites.

CHAPTER 6:

DAY #2

Day #2 is either Thursday or Friday, depending on your schedule. Pick a day that tends to work best for you, and block out either morning from 9am-11am for 40 weeks of your year! During those two hours, you are going to spend more time marketing your open house and solidifying your neighborhood presence.

I'd like to begin with a disclaimer. In the past, Craigslist ads were a hugely successful tactic to procure open house traffic. My formula was to post Wednesday, Friday and Sunday mornings about my open house. I loved Craigslist because it was free and open house visitors would attribute their attendance to my ads. Unfortunately, due to spammers, scammers and creeps, I have decided to phase out this tactic. So, please take the next step at your comfort level.

Determine if Craigslist is an effective tool in your

region. If you use Craigslist, invite people to your open house and point them to your blog to discover more details about the neighborhood – don't let the ad be the end-game, let it lead people to learn more about you and to connect with you.

There are more sites than Craigslist for non-listing agents to post open houses ads – your local newspaper's online edition, for example – just make sure that you have the listing agent's approval to do so. If the listing agent already posted the open house on these sites, your ad could create confusion with consumers (unlike Craigslist where redundancy is beneficial). Some sites like Postlets.com produce beautiful ads, but may have rules about posting someone else's listing. Be careful not to syndicate your ad to the other major sites like Zillow or Trulia – the site could assume you are the new listing agent and wipe out the actual listing agent's post.

In the past, I encouraged agents do *all* their online ads on Day #1, giving them more days to gather leads. But since that day is already jam-packed, I've given you a slight break so you don't feel like your head is underwater on Tuesdays. Also note, many of these online open house notices are taken care of when the listing agent enters the open house into the MLS system and the information is syndicated to participating sites. Contact your MLS board to learn more about where your listings have syndication agreements.

Budget-Friendly Farming

Let's talk about how you can get the effects of the farming mail-out, but on a tighter budget. Perhaps you have the means to do the mail-out, but prefer the following method. You know yourself the best, so choose what works best for you!

The steps are simple on this day: take that exact same letter from the previous chapter, print it 200 times, and then place them on the front doors of the 200 neighbors that you would've mailed to. Ta-da!

I'm going to brag for a moment, not only am I lucky enough to work for a company that is agent-centered instead of company-centered, and where I have been able to fine tune this open house system over the years due to our collaborative nature, my company provides free black and white copies at the office! I know all you agents reading this can appreciate what I just said, so I'll say it again: *free* black and white copies at the office! Lucky, right?! I'm sorry if you are not as lucky as me, but do not despair. At places like Office Depot, you can get 200 copies for $0.09/page! That's only $18 to flyer 200 homes. Correction: that's only $18 to market yourself to 200 homes with a valid reason (remember, you're not sending out pie recipes, you are inviting them to an event where they can get valuable information and even win a gift card!). When else do you have a better excuse to market to a neighborhood than when you have an open house? Your $18 is well-spent here, believe me!

After you've printed your flyers, set out to paper the neighborhood. You will want to dress comfortably, but professionally – remember, first impressions are key! And please, learn from my mistakes, do not wear high-heels while papering 200 homes! Master the comfortable-yet-professional look, so that when you run into neighbors, you don't feel like ducking in a bush to hide from them!

Choose a time to walk the neighborhood with flyers when you won't be getting in people's way as they are backing out of their driveway to race to work; and you'll want to get started before the day starts heating up (either with the sun or with buyers ready to look at houses!).

Your goal here is to run into neighbors *casually* and add the human element of inviting them to your open house. I've had friendly waves from garages to thirty-minute conversations about real estate by flower beds. Welcome the opportunities that this walk brings you and grow your database by everyone that you speak to.

Did a light bulb just pop up over your head? If you're thinking what I'm thinking, you're going to send each person you spoke with on your walk a handwritten note later today to tell them how much you enjoyed your conversation and (based on how your conversation went) that you either look forward to seeing them at the open house or you want to be sure they have the materials they are going to miss since they cannot come to the open house. And, this person just got ADDED TO YOUR DATABASE!

In your database management system, be sure to have different tags or groups that organize your contacts. For example, you'd want to move someone you spoke with on your neighborhood walk from the general farming group, to 'people I've met.' Have a group of contacts for each open house address so that you know who and how to follow up!

If a physical ailment prevents you from walking the neighborhood, employ someone else (your kid, a neighborhood kid with their parents' permission, an assistant). Even though you will miss out on the opportunity to bump into some of the neighbors and introduce yourself, ideally striking up a conversation about real estate, you will get another chance at the open house to speak with them. Regardless, your name is getting out in front of them, and that is what is important here.

The benefits of going door-to-door are the same as described with the letter in the preceding chapter; however, you gain the ability to get face time with your farm, and you can't put a price tag on that! You even get a little exercise to boot!

Be sure to have a couple extra flyers on hand to give to any local business owners. Ask if they will let you hang your flyer in their window or designated display area. Perhaps they know someone interested in moving to the neighborhood, too? They can even give you extra insight into the neighborhood that you can pass along to your open house visitors. Let them know about your giveaway – perhaps they'll donate gift cards or coupons! Add these business owners to your database!

Key Notes:

⇨Continue ramping up your marketing efforts throughout the week for maximum leads – this includes leads who may not be able to come to the open house.

⇨Online ads and door-to-door flyers are inexpensive yet effective ways to reach leads.

⇨Grow your database with everyone you meet – including local business owners.

CHAPTER 7:

DAY #3

Welcome to the weekend! All real estate agents know what this means – it's busy time! Weekends are when people fly into town to house hunt and have time off from work to meet us on listing appointments. And, of course, it's the optimal time for your open houses!

Again, we're going with the assumption that your open house is on Sunday, making Day #3 Saturday. If your open house is Saturday instead, you'll add in Day #4 to this day and have Sunday to relax (unless you're doubling up of course!).

Speaking of that word – relax – be sure to schedule some you-time today! Down time/family time/happy hour/date night – whatever it is that makes you happy, work it into your schedule so that you don't leave the weekend feeling more frazzled than you did coming into the weekend. If you don't take time for yourself, burnout is inevitable.

You are only going to spend a little time today to prepare for tomorrow's open house. I suggest doing these steps in the morning so you can spend the rest of the day with clients or having you-time. If you wait to prepare for your open house until nightfall, you risk not getting it done at all. Besides, I'd rather relax at night, wouldn't you?

Many of these items below are something you can prepare once and reuse for each open house. Keep a running inventory of these items on your computer so you can optimize your time on Saturday morning. You should be able to make a couple of changes, print, and go! You'll also need folders, preferably ones that are personally branded, for these items to go into. These handouts are called your **Pieces of Value (POV)**:

⇨ Market Update – this is printed on your letterhead and details the climate of the overall market right now. Include stats such as current interest rates, information on FHA loan limits, job growth and population growth for your city, median home prices in your city, and city-wide months of inventory. Many times your favorite title company sales rep has a list of these stats compiled for you and you can easily transfer them to your letterhead. You can keep a running stock of this flyer, fact-checking the data once a month. Your call-to-action (CTA): at the bottom of the flyer, invite them to coffee with you to discuss the market. *"Let's get together over coffee to discuss in detail what these stats mean to you as either a homebuyer or seller!"*

Bonus: when you prepare your update, the statistics become fresh in your mind and you'll sound more knowledgeable at your open house!

You will add this to both your buyer and seller folders.

⇨ Open house flyer – you already have the financial flyer from the lender that has the first two or three MLS pictures and basic stats of the home, but you will also want to do a flyer that captures the house info *and* neighborhood info. The goal is to get far-reaching with as little material as possible – provide value without over-loading your guests with information. On this flyer, have a small paragraph about the basic stats on the house, and be sure to include tax and HOA amounts since buyers like to ask questions about those at open houses.

Instead of putting pictures of the home, put a market snapshot of the active listings in the neighborhood. Below this information, add in more details about the neighborhood, such as: inventory, recent sold data, pending data and actives data. The beauty of preparing this information the day before the open house is that you will now have up-to-date knowledge of the neighborhood and can sound informed during your open house conversations. When a visitor asks you, "What are homes selling for around here?" you won't reply with "Uhhhhh..."!

Don't forget your contact information and CTA on this flyer! On the back of the flyer, print out all of the other available homes and the CTA to schedule appointments to see these homes with YOU! At your open house you will point this CTA out to prospective buyers, helping to solidify you as the go-to agent in their minds. Also, be sure to mention the FSBOs you've made contact with so that buyers understand that you can represent them with those homes as well.

You will also want to put this POV in your seller folders, to educate potential sellers about their competition – this comes in handy when you go to the listing appointment and they already have realistic values in mind because of your handout.

⇨ Tips For Preparing Your Home For Sale – you can find detailed lists on how to prepare a home for the market almost anywhere – from online to the back page of your CMAs. Compile the tips into a list on your letterhead or into a brochure and keep a steady stock so you can grab and go! These go in your seller folders.

⇨ Feedback Form – have a feedback form saved on your computer and

For templates of these POV, visit:
ShannonEnsor.com/yktohs/resources

ready to go at all times. Before each open house, you will simply need to clarify the prize for the drawing and hit print. On the top half of this form you will have questions about the house and allow the visitor to rank them on a scale of one to five. On the bottom half of this form, remind them of the gift card drawing (I suggest $50 because it entices your visitors to fill out their correct information, whereas a smaller amount may not) and ask for their complete contact information, including phone number, email and home address. I find this a good spot to ask for their Realtor's name (I don't simply ask yes/no, I want to know the name!).

⇨ You need several clipboards so that you can have several feedback forms on each one. Now, you are ready to hand these out to people as they tour your home. (Don't forget the pens!) I will explain in the next chapter how this is a more successful system for increasing your database than having them sign into a ledger.

⇨ Be sure that your lender has dropped off the co-branded financial flyers to you that you asked for on Tuesday. Add them to your buyer folders.

Now that you have all of your POV ready to go, assemble them into your branded folders, along with your business card and a brochure about yourself. You will have two stacks of folders – one that you will hand out to prospective buyers and one that you will hand out to prospective sellers and nosy neighbors.

Notice that I did not say, "Have as many stacks of all the handouts from the title company as possible"? Nor do you need to burden yourself with relocation packets and tons of other material.

While out showing homes to a buyer one day, we came across a property on her list that was being held open. This was a small condo, but it had an updated kitchen with great counter space going for it. However, we could barely see this counter space through all of the open house agent's handouts. She must've felt super-prepared that day setting up for her open house as she laid out nearly 20 stacks of papers all over the kitchen countertop and bar space! Want to guess what kind of information she had out? Each stack was a different print-out from a local title company. '101 Things To Do in Austin', 'Austin's Best Shopping Districts' and 'Kids Activities' were among the titles. All of these were branded to the title company and none were branded to the agent.

The agent probably didn't care that my client wasn't interested in the home, since she was not the listing agent, but what about her other open house visitors? When Brenda Buyer walks into an open house like this, she will walk away with tons of glossy material from the title company and maybe that agent's business card. She wonders later what a title company is and how she got the business card that landed between her car seat and console.

Be wise in what you pass out to your visitors. Give them strategic POVs, as found in the list above, and make sure they are all in color and high-quality paper and are neatly stuffed into your branded folder. Why color and high-quality paper vs. black & white on cheap copy paper (this isn't your listing after all)? Because every piece of information you hand to visitors is a reflection of YOU.

Why do I keep mentioning the branded folders? Two reasons: 1) people are less likely to toss out a functional folder and if you're branded on the front, you'll have more ways of popping up in their eyesight; and 2) you'll tell them at the open house that you'll be sending them more information, so they should save the folder and keep it all together – now they have a connection to you and expectation to receive more information from you (such as those glossy title handouts that talk about school ratings or estimated closing costs...or the MLS sheets for the homes you'll see together the following week!).

If you visit two open houses and at one take away some generic glossy material about the city and at the other you get pieces of value and are told to hold on to the folder because more pieces of value are coming your way, which agent do you think you will feel more enticed to work with?

This leads me to another point. You don't want to give your open house visitors the moon *and* the stars at the open house. Instead, you want to leave open the opportunity to send them more information. For example, if a couple walks into your open house and alludes to being avid golfers, instead of handing them the title company's printout of 'Top Area Golf Courses', take this as an excuse to follow-up with them after the open house with more information: "I'm going to send you a great resource I have that maps all the top golf courses in the area! Let me make sure I have your best email address to send that to you when I'm done with my open house."

Now, not only do you have an excuse to contact them after the open house, you are confirming that you haven't been given a fake email address. I cannot count the amount of times when people perk up, meaning I can actually see their walls coming down, and say, "Actually, that's my work address (pointing to where they signed in with john.doe@yahoo.com). My home address would be better: ...." (now the 'doe' is gone and a much more believable email address is given)!

This small amount of time you spend on Saturday morning prepares you for your Sunday open house so that you have everything ready to go and are not running around frantically right before your open house. It helps you get ahead of any printing blunders (like running out of ink an hour before your open house). You're also more mentally prepared since you've studied up on the recent statistics for the neighborhood. You can now walk into your open house tomorrow feeling confident!

Key Notes:

⇨Only give guests Pieces of Value that are branded to you and increases *your* value in their eyes.

⇨Every POV should have a CTA (Call to Action).

⇨Don't forget about YOU time.

CHAPTER 8:

OPEN HOUSE DAY!

You've spent your week advertising and preparing for your open house and now it is show time!

The first thing you need to do is one more advertising push on your Facebook business account. Same goes for your Craigslist ad, if you're implementing that tactic. This morning-of push will grab people as they get their house-hunting game plan in order over their morning coffee. Optimize the amount of leads you receive and think of your advertising strategy as a one-two punch. First you hit them throughout the week with the online ads you began on Tuesday and Thursday, and now you hit them again Sunday morning when the open house is imminent.

Assuming you are freshly showered and are wearing one of your best outfits, you are now ready to grab the material you prepared yesterday, carefully load your signs into your trunk and head to the bakery or store to grab your refreshments and balloons.

You want to already have a game plan in mind for what you plan to get from the bakery. (Maybe you serve the same thing every week and are known as the agent who always has cronuts at their open house!) Knowing ahead of time allows you to plan any serving trays, cups, utensils, paper napkins, and other necessary items. I also like to bring, with owner permission, a higher-end candle (in a seasonal or popular scent that smells of home-baked goods – ask others for their opinion on the scent in case you don't have a nose for offending smells) and a lighter.

You know yourself best! If you are the type of person who is notoriously late to everything, you may want to grab your refreshments on Saturday – just be sure that you are also not the type who would be tempted to eat the refreshments overnight!

> Be sure to discuss with your CPA how your open house expenses can be deducted from your annual tax return.

I urge you to make exciting choices for your open house treats. Anyone can bring the boring chocolate chip cookies from the grocery store. Separate yourself from your competition! Go to a bakery or specialty store and grab something that will stand out to your visitors. You will want to set your budget based on the type of home you are holding open – doughnuts will not do at a luxury listing (unless they come from the high-end, super-popular bakery located near the neighborhood and are accompanied by a fruit tray, chicken salad croissants and mimosas). Get creative with your refreshments: some bakeries do personalized or house-shaped sugar cookies, or you can serve muffins instead of cookies, or have a wine and cheese assortment. Let your refreshment choices say to visitors that you are not an ordinary agent – you are the agent who pays attention to detail and goes above and beyond for your clients!

Success tip: Buy a small helium tank from a party store to save on your balloon costs.

I know there are some of you right now who are still stuck on the b-word I mentioned a few paragraphs ago: balloons. I have never come across a more controversial tool in the real estate world! I know that many people object to them for environmental issues. If this is you, please find a substitute. The point is to not have naked directional signs. Balloons signal to house hunters that your open house is fresh and going on *now*, not yesterday or last week. There are some companies that have balloon stakes that allow you to reuse the same balloon each week and you forgo helium. Pinwheels and flags are also good. Find your method that works best for *you*. While you are at it, don't forget to dress up the sign in the yard of the home!

Now that you have your gear ready to go, arrive in your recently-washed vehicle to the open house at least 45 minutes before start time. Be sure that the sellers understand that you are coming early and not right at the open house start time. One time I assumed the sellers knew I would be at their home early for set-up – let's just say they thought they had time for the "smoke to clear" by the time I arrived! It was an embarrassing situation for all – don't let that happen to you!

When you surveyed the neighborhood and property on Tuesday, you would have noticed if any barriers to entry exist for yourself and the open house visitors. Address those barriers ahead of time and have a system in place so that visitors can easily access your open house. For example, if the house or condo is gate-guarded, speak with the guard about your open house and see if you can leave flyers with directions to your house/unit for them to give to interested guests. No guard, but you have a gate to contend with? Get HOA approval to put a sign on the keypad with your phone number, telling visitors to text you for the access code. Bonus: when visitors text you, you now have their phone number and can enter them into your database, even if they forget to add their phone number to your sign-in sheet!

When you arrive at the home, the first thing you need to do is remove any flyers from the flyer box outside the home. Now, buyers must walk *inside* your open house for information about the home. Just be sure to replace the flyers when you leave or you will have one angry listing agent on your hands!

Next, set up your materials. Pick the room in the house that makes the most sense when it comes to attractiveness, space and seating options. Most times this is the breakfast room or the area adjacent to the kitchen. In Texas, it's common to have a floor plan with the formal dining room near the entry of the home. I steer away from setting up in this formal dining space if I can, so that I'm not hitting my visitors with my POV the moment they walk through the door. I like for them to walk through the house and to the kitchen/breakfast area to get to the material so that we've had time to warm up to each other. I'll explain more on this conversation flow in a bit.

Let's say for our open house today we have a nicely staged home with a bright breakfast room across from the kitchen. On the dining table, thoughtfully line up your buyer folders, seller folders, and clipboards on the side where visitors will be nearest first. In the center of the table, yet within easy reach, make an eye-appealing display of your refreshments. Stash any of your personal belongings in a cabinet and make sure to hide them well. Do not have any other extra clutter on the table. You don't want to distract your visitors from the home, or from your POV and sign-in sheets.

In the beginning of my open house career I would bake chocolate chip cookies in the oven right before the open house started. You can even put a couple of drops of vanilla on a baking dish in the oven for that freshly-baked cookie smell. If either method appeals to you, be sure to check the oven before preheating it! Homeowners store all kinds of things in their ovens, including their plastic Tupperware – don't learn this lesson the hard way! Also, be mindful of the oven over-heating the kitchen and making your guests uncomfortable, especially in the summer. I now prefer to buy my goodies from the bakery and have a candle that mimics freshly baked goods. Whichever route you go, make sure you have ample time to prepare.

Now is also the time to adjust the thermostats to the appropriate setting so that your guests will be comfortable. But first, take note of what the homeowner has the thermostat set to, this way you can set it right back when you leave. If you have homeowner approval, light a fire in the fireplace so that you can show off this feature of the home. Next, turn on all of the lights in the home, including lamps, and raise the blinds to the appropriate height (making sure to close any blinds that help conceal ugly views). Do a quick run inside (and outside!) the home to make sure all rooms look tidy, paying close attention to countertops and floor space. I've had to remove decoy snakes from doorways and hide dirty laundry piles before!

Tip: Have two bar stools that are counter height to bring to your vacant open houses – then you can set up shop at the kitchen counter and not be forced to stand all day!

After the home is ready, and with about 30 minutes remaining before your open house, you will now venture out to place your directionals. I advise against setting up your signs any earlier. The directionals are meant to lead visitors to your *open* house. Don't anger them by leading them to a closed house – or worse, to the seller who will be tempted to give them a tour themselves.

Be sure to lock the house when you leave to put out your directionals! You don't want any unwanted guests while the house is unattended.

Pull out the map you made on Tuesday and start with the furthest point from the home and work your way in. If on Tuesday you had to leave your letter on a door, you'll either find that your letter was taken (and they didn't call to object to your sign in the yard) or that it is still there (signaling either they are out of town, or they don't check their door often – it's okay for you to go ahead and put your sign in their yard respectfully, they'll come across your letter eventually).

Pay attention to these next words and engrave them on your memory. As you are putting your directionals out, HAVE A SMILE ON YOUR FACE!!!! People are watching you. They are watching from their living room windows. They are watching you from their cars as they drive by. They see you laboring to put the sign in the ground – a time when a smile is the last thing you want to have on your face. You may have sweat dripping from your forehand, but by golly, be smiling!

Even if you're not the one putting the signs out, tell your assistant or whomever you have hired, to always wear a smile when they are outside. They are an extension of you.

You may not know when you are giving a first impression, but you only have the one shot. Don't make people think twice about visiting your open house or calling you for a listing appointment because they saw you grumbling while doing your job. (They are receiving all of your material and see that you are actively working their neighborhood, so you should be on their list of agents to call by now! Don't counteract your hard work with a bad attitude!)

Put your final directional in the yard of the home you are holding open, making sure to attach extra balloons to this sign. You should now have about five to ten minutes to wipe the sweat from your brow and refresh yourself. Take three deep, yoga-like breaths, and open the door – it's show time!

Show Time!

Up to this point you have spent five to six days marketing online through ads and blogs, marketing to drive-by traffic through your open house sign rider, and marketing through letters or flyers that you have sent to the neighborhood. You are generating leads, growing your database and building credibility as the neighborhood expert. Buyers, sellers and referral sources have seen your efforts.

When someone walks into the door of your open house, your steps will be to:

⇨ knock down any communication barriers they

present

⇨ build rapport

⇨ learn which of the three types of visitors they are (buyer, seller or referral source)

Your desired goal with each visitor is to engage them in one of the following:

⇨ writing a contract on the home you are holding open

⇨ becoming their buyer's agent for another home

⇨ listing their home for sale

⇨ receiving a referral so that you can perform one of the above steps for another lead

Can you sense the presence of great business opportunities ahead of you at this open house? Now, more than ever, is your time to shine!

> *Everyone* that walks through the door is an opportunity to grow your database.

We've discussed your look and the look of the open house you are presenting. You are beyond prepared to discuss the neighborhood and housing market with your guests (and it wouldn't hurt to be caught up on current events as extra icebreaker-ammunition). There are two more tools you need to have in your arsenal: your smile and ability to listen. Really! Once you have the look and preparedness down, those are your key tools for the rest of the open house.

Smile and the Whole World Smiles with You

Smiles are contagious. Smiles represent warmth. Service with a smile is preached at every customer service job, and for good reason.

When people walk into your open house they are on high-alert. Picture a stereotypical used car salesperson represented in TV commercials. They are loud, obnoxious and exude cheesiness and artificial flattery. Of course, this is a tactic used by commercial producers to grab your attention and have their brand stick out in your mind. Sadly, open house visitors project that exact same image onto real estate agents – as if it's a general salesperson trait. As they walk up to your open house they are mentally preparing to be met by the used car salesman type, fake smile in tow. They are going to do everything in their power to duck and dodge you (unless they are a neighbor who received your invitation, of course).

Alter their expectation by greeting them with a genuine smile instead. You are genuine, aren't you? You genuinely want to grow your real estate business and wouldn't be reading this book if you weren't. You have the knowledge and tools to help people buy or sell their homes. And wouldn't you know it, here they are walking into a *home* – your product! They have a need (whether it is buying this weekend or selling in six months) and you have the ability to help them meet that need. Therefore, when you open the door to greet your guest, I want you to mentally say each time in your head, *"Hello, I'm here to help you. How can we get started?"* and give them the genuine smile that will naturally come to your face. (If a smile does not naturally come to your face when you say that sentence, you may be in the wrong profession!)

Of course, that is not the sentence you will say out loud. Instead, I want you to introduce yourself: "Hi, I'm Shannon," and reach your hand out to them and WAIT for their response. Hold eye contact and really wait for them to respond. Make them fill the silence with telling you their name. Unless they completely lack social skills, they will respond with their *correct* first name and introduce anyone with them as well. You are off to a good start.

Examples of agents who are not off to a good start include the agent who doesn't introduce himself, but leads with, "Hi, welcome to the open house. This house has three bedrooms and ...". That agent has lost the guest. The guest is now tearing her way through the home, discovering how many bedrooms it has on her own. Slow down the interaction and make it about, *"Hi, I'm a human being who is smiling and reaching my hand out to you as a respectful gesture to another human being.*" This approach shows the guest that you are genuinely interested in meeting them, not in throwing them a sales pitch.

Guess who else is not off to a good start? If you answered the agent who doesn't even greet their guest, then not only are you correct but you are guessing what I see happen more times than not.

Make note, I'm not calling out the agent who is so busy at an open house that he cannot even keep up with greeting everyone who walks through the door – although, doesn't that sound like a fun position to be in? That agent gets a pass because the visitor senses his busyness and should receive a warm greeting as soon as the agent politely excuses himself from the first visitor. Visitors are oftentimes intrigued by an agent's perceived success and will vie for the agent's attention if they are serious prospects. This is the "everyone else wanted to talk to him, so I'll be missing out if I don't" phenomenon. Learn to balance your time between guests, so that they all receive your attention.

No, I'm talking about the agent who doesn't even make the effort to greet the guests. I've seen it way too many times to count. I like to pop into other people's open houses with my agent thinking-cap on. To my surprise, more often than not, I'm met by an apathetic agent who doesn't even acknowledge my entry. One time, the agent was ASLEEP at the kitchen table! Another time, the agent refused to remove her nose from a sultry (non-real estate related) novel! If you were a prospective buyer or a seller who was out to interview agents, would you have chosen those agents? I know my answer is a resounding "no"!

I ask the agents who don't greet me with a smile what their position is. I want to know: am I dealing with an assistant, listing agent or hopeful buyers' agent? The assistants are the only ones who get a 'pass' for not putting forth the effort (although I certainly would not feel that way if I were their boss!). When I learn that it is indeed an agent who is holding the house open, I know one thing: that this poor agent thinks their only duty is to unlock the door and waste three hours of their weekend. This agent is oblivious to the true powers of an open house. They don't realize that they can gain neighborhood credibility, buyer/seller/referral leads, and database growth from a properly performed open house. No wonder they aren't rushing to the door to greet me with a smile!

Realize the amplitude of open houses and how they can elevate your business to whole new success levels, and you will have a hard time wiping your smile off your face when someone knocks on the door!

Two Ears and One Mouth

Some agents mistake talking a lot for building credibility. They think that the more stats they can rattle off about a home, and the more they talk *to* the visitor, the better. They think *their words* are inducing the visitor to work with them, but they couldn't be further from the truth. Their open house interaction looks similar to this:

Agent: "Hi! Welcome to 123 Elm Street! Come on in and take a look at this beautiful 1950s home with three bedrooms and two full baths. This is a single story home and you'll just love the flat backyard. It's a great find for only $300,000. Please let me know if you have any questions!"

Potential Buyer (thinks to self): "Well, I no longer have any questions, because you just answered them all. I need a four-bedroom house, so now I know I should go down the street to the other open house. I'm going to walk around just so this doesn't seem awkward and duck out the door as soon as possible."

The agent is confused when the visitor high-tails it out of the house 45 seconds later. *"Didn't he love my sentence about this house being a great find?!"*

What happened in the scenario above? The agent left no room for listening to or connecting with the visitor. She didn't ask about the potential buyer's needs. Instead, she blurted out several sentences requiring no interaction with the buyer. The buyer determined his needs were not met with this home, and he promptly went on to the next open house.

While this book is not about agent scripts, as there are many great books on this subject, including Tom Hopkins' *Mastering the Art of Selling Real Estate*, I want to touch on how your introductory conversation with your open house visitors should go instead. We'll pick up after the visitors, a couple this time, have given their names.

Agent: "Nice to meet you, (Buyers' names). What brings you out house-hunting today?"

Agent *listens* for answer.

Buyer (the wife): "Oh, we're just starting our home search and are trying to get an idea about different neighborhoods."

Agent: "Oh, that's great! Why don't you take a look around and when you get to the kitchen, I have some information about this neighborhood that I think you'll find helpful, as well as some refreshments!"

116

The agent said all of this with a genuine smile and actually listened to what the potential buyers had to say – not pretend to listen so that the conversation can be taken back over with her bedroom-to-bathroom-ratio knowledge of the house. Now the agent knows key information about the buyers, and the buyers do not feel overwhelmed by the agent. The buyers are able to relax and view the house in peace, knowing that the agent doesn't fall into the high-pressure salesperson category.

As the buyers meander their way through the house, they come upon the kitchen. They notice the elegant display of refreshments and the two professional stacks of folders. The agent greets them again and hands a clipboard and pen to the wife, since she exuded more warmth and openness when they met at the door.

Agent: "The sellers really look forward to your feedback on the house, and we are sure to keep your evaluations anonymous. Be sure to fill out the contact information completely so you can be in the drawing for the $50 gift card!"

Let's break down the mechanics of what has taken place so far:

⇨ The agent allowed the couple to relax and feel unpressured as they made their way to the kitchen. She gauged their personalities from their initial meeting and decided who would be more open and forthcoming on the contact/feedback sheet. She made a quick evaluation that if she handed the sheet to the husband who was more hesitant to shake her hand, she may not receive a complete form back.

⇨ Then, she commented that the sellers are interested in the feedback of the home (which of course, they are). This is using the power of a third-party (who is the absentee seller allowing the visitors an inside-look into their personal life). You're shifting focus from you wanting the feedback to the seller wanting it – or in other words, shifting from the salesperson they may still be leery of to the third-party that they'll likely never meet, yet owe some feedback to since they are about to check out their bedroom closets!

⇨ The agent mentions the anonymity so that the visitors feel comfortable being honest on the form. Now, they don't feel awkward about putting their contact info and their honest rating of the home on the sheet.

⇨ On top of keeping things low-pressure, she is potentially rewarding them for their visit! Everyone loves a chance to win something – especially if it is a nice enough sum (thus, why I suggest $50 instead of $20). In the grand scheme of things, spending $50 to get quality leads at an open house is way cheaper than what many lead-generating companies and advertising outlets charge you. And, we're talking leads you have built rapport with versus cold leads!

With their task at hand, and motivation to see the rest of the home, the potential buyers continue through the home, making sure to give evaluations on the sheet provided to them on the clipboard.

The agent stays behind to greet other guests and will occasionally pop-in to check on the couple as they tour the home, making sure to point out any of the home's features. She builds trust with them by not breathing down their necks while showing she's available for questions. She encourages them to talk about their thoughts on the rooms, instead of making the show about *her*.

Once the couple has completed their tour, they return to the agent to give back the clipboard. She quickly skims the section where the form asks if they are working with another agent – that's the only section they have left blank, so she makes a mental note to work it into their conversation in a moment.

Here comes serious rapport-building time! The last thing she wants is that couple to dart out the door without her having a conversation with them. This is when the two ears and one mouth really kick in. She'll be sure to ask questions that elicit long, informative answers from the couple – avoiding questions that could only receive a yes/no response.

Bad Examples:

Agent: "Do you like this house?" "Does it fit in your budget?" "Is the floor plan good for your family?"

These conversation-killing questions only leave room for "yes" or "no" answers. When conversation falls flat, guests feel prompted to exit the home, feeling as though the agent never got to know them. They feel no connection to that agent and the chance of them calling them for representation becomes slim.

Good Examples:

Agent: "How does this floor plan compare to other homes that you've looked at?" "Would you do anything differently in this home design-wise?" "What are the issues with the home that would prevent you from making an offer?" "What are your favorite features of this home?"

All of these questions get the buyer to open up and allow the listening agent to learn more about their wants, needs and readiness to buy. When an agent identifies someone's wants, needs and readiness to buy, and focuses their conversation on those items, the potential client will begin to feel a connection with that agent. They'll definitely feel much more connected than if they simply answered yes or no to a few questions! This connectedness is the rapport building you are looking for and will result in representation agreements.

Back to our scenario, the agent then hands them a folder she knows is from her buyers stack. Conversation is flowing, leading the agent to open the folder to either the page about other homes for sale in the neighborhood and the price-per-square-foot statistics, or to the lender information. More value-added question-and-answer time follows.

Through intentional listening skills, the agent carefully crafts each subsequent question to evoke a revealing answer about the couple's real estate needs – with the conclusion coming to either the agent writing an offer on the house for them, or meeting them another time to look at more homes together.

If the agent learns that the couple is just browsing homes and cannot buy for another six months, then she changes up her tactics and makes sure she has their correct email addresses so that she can upload their wants and needs into her MLS system and send them daily or weekly reports with matching homes. They are clearly interested in how the market is doing, since they are visiting open houses, so they will appreciate the market updates, even if they are not ready to buy this month.

If she would have identified them as a potential seller instead, she would've given them a seller packet and led the conversation toward a pre-listing appointment – using open-ended questions, of course!

The key in every situation is to learn how you can work together – moving forward from the open house to the next step in your leads' real estate paths.

When a Dead End Isn't a Dead End

I've heard agents say that the path stops as soon as they learn the visitor is represented by another agent. They clam up and give the cold shoulder – some because they think they've hit a dead-end, others because they are scared of stepping on toes.

I stand firmly with the REALTOR Code of Ethics and say to never *ever* poach another agent's clients. And, it is easy to avoid stepping on toes as long as you are not violating the Code of Ethics (this includes not bad-mouthing the other agent or telling the visitor to dump their agent and go with you!).

However, don't ignore someone just because they have an agent. Instead, impress them with your professionalism and courtesy. You never know, they may think their agent is too busy for referrals and they'll gladly send referrals your way in lieu of getting their personal business!

Leave a good impression on everyone that walks through the doorway and see what comes of it – you will be pleasantly surprised when referrals come your way, and you'll feel much better about your attitude at the open house!

All About Attitude

Speaking of attitude, if you have a bad run-in at your open house – for instance, you have the visitor that speeds through and no matter how kind and easy-going you are, still avoids you as if you were a ghost and then exits the home

If your nerves start creeping in or you can't find your way out of a conversational lull, distract yourself and the visitor by offering the refreshments – they make great icebreakers.

without a measly "hi" – don't let that affect your attitude when the next visitor comes. Shake it off, take some deep breaths and clear the bad encounter out of your mind. While there is no guarantee that everyone that walks through your door will be a nice person – there are many reasons for this, including anxiety disorders – you can make a pact with yourself to recover gracefully when it does happen. Just like each open house is different from the other, so are your open house guests. Snap back to happy after a bad encounter so that your subsequent guests don't suffer – and you don't suffer by missing leads.

This leads me to reiterate a point I've made several times in this book: if you've had a slow open house, maybe even one with zero visitors, don't let that carry into your next open house! There are going to be great open houses and bad ones, but your attitude has to stay consistently good through them all.

If you feel yourself getting burnt out, take off for a weekend and do something to recharge. Read a motivational book or unwind your mind at a movie. You must get yourself out of the slump so you can continue on to your goals of capturing neighborhood credibility, getting leads and growing your database. No one in a slump can achieve those goals.

Early in my real estate career I had a run of slow open houses. One particular Sunday morning I had every *excuse* in the world to back out of the open house I had planned, including a hangover. However, I decided to stick to my commitment and I gathered up every ounce of happy I could muster.

When I arrived to my open house, around noon, the

rain started pouring. It poured on and off for the duration of my open house. No one was coming to my open house. I felt like I was wasting my time when I would much rather be at home nursing my headache! With about 20 minutes left in the open house, a knock at the door finally came.

Long story short, that visitor was relocating her company to Austin and not only did she need to buy a home, quite a few other families in her company needed an agent as well! I went from hopeless, to procuring several closings – all at one rainy open house during my "slump".

If I would've allowed my bad attitude take over, I never would have received all of that business from that one "slow" open house. In fact, that business came at a crucial make-or-break time in my career. Are you facing a period in your career where you wonder if you can even make it as an agent? Take it from me, press on with your open houses and always have a good attitude – you too can rise above a slump!

Side note: I believe rainy days are great days for an open house. When the weather is bad, the buyers must be serious! Don't let bad weather deter you from success!

Open House Success Tips:

⇨ After each guest leaves, write notes about what you learned about them on the back of the feedback/contact form. It can be hard to put faces and stories to names after you meet 20 or so couples during a three-hour span, so these notes will come in handy when you reach out to your guests (aka your leads) again. This information will help you be more personal in the thank you notes you will write to them later, and it helps you to give better feedback to the listing agent.

⇨ When no one is in your open house, keep yourself busy, but with real-estate related tasks. Writing thank you notes and reading a business-building book are great ways to pass the time. Whatever you do, don't get caught slacking off!

One time I peeked in on a listing of mine that was being held open by an agent I had never met. The house was a new, custom build, and it was staged quite nicely. The way the house was laid out, you could not see someone walk in if you were sitting at the kitchen table.

When I turned the corner to the kitchen/living room area, my jaw hit the ground. The agent had newspapers spread out spanning the entire granite kitchen counter top, down to the stained-concrete floor and out into the living room. It was as though he was mimicking a trail of ants through the house with his unbelievably large stack of newspapers! It turns out, he uses his open house time to call his bookies and get all of his bets in! He apparently could not be bothered by anyone's presence, as he barely lifted his eyes to acknowledge me. I was in shock.

Only after I introduced myself as the listing agent did he start to scramble and pick up all of the papers. Could you imagine what a homebuyer would think of this situation? Could you imagine a potential seller wanting to hire *him* as their listing agent after this? Can you imagine the conversation I had with him next?! Needless to say, he was never allowed to hold open any of my listings again. I didn't stay with that brokerage much longer, either.

⇨ Keep your goals in mind during your open house. Have "4 X 40 = 160" written on a note card that you bring in your briefcase to your open houses. Reminding yourself of your greater goal will help you through the slower periods and make you feel accomplished each time you fly past four visitors.

Key Notes:

⇨Best time to remind people of your open house through your online advertising is on the morning-of the open house.

⇨The more you have prepared for your open house the day-before, the more calm and confident you will be at your open house.

⇨Everything you present at your open house reflects upon your professionalism. Even dessert details can help elevate you above your competition.

⇨Make it easy for guests to find your open house – attract them through the use of balloons, etc.

⇨Strategize the perfect flow of your open house for superior conversation opportunities with your guests.

⇨Smile! And take deep breaths.

⇨Your initial goals: break down communication barriers, build rapport and learn what type of lead source each guest is.

⇨Your ultimate goals: writing a contract on the open house listing, or becoming their buyer's agent for another home, and/or becoming their listing agent, and receiving referrals.

⇨Greet *all* of your guests with a genuine smile. Be sincere in finding out how you can help them.

⇨Ask questions with open-ended answers to learn the most about your guest and build rapport.

⇨Let tenacity and a good attitude pull you through slow periods in your career.

CHAPTER 9:

AFTER THE OPEN HOUSE

Congratulations, you are 2/3^{rds} done with your open house! If you previously lived your real estate career where your open house ended as soon as you picked up your signs, you are going to have an epiphany by the end of this chapter.

Obviously your first steps will be to shut down the open house – this means turning off lights, blowing out candles (make sure you do this with enough time to let them cool if you are bringing the candles home with you), resetting the thermostat, turning blinds back to how you found them, and cleaning up after yourself so the owner can hardly tell you were there. Be sure to leave the house locked the way it was when you arrived – many people rely on their house-to-garage door being unlocked when they get home, so be mindful of how they left the house to you and don't lock them out!

Before you leave to pick up your signs, think about what to do with your leftover refreshments, if you have any. Is there a fire or police station nearby that you can drop them by with your co-branded lender flyers that have information about special loan programs for community workers? If not, consider dropping a plate of refreshments off at the homes that allowed you to have your sign in their yard all day. Be intentional with everything you do, and put those refreshments to good use instead of on your hips!

Once your signs are picked up, do you have any buyer or pre-listing appointments to attend? If so, be sure to leave yourself some time to grab any information off your computer, and a snack so you won't be working on an empty stomach!

If you don't have any appointments set up, think back to any promises you may have made to your open house guests. Did you tell someone you'd set them up on a MLS search tonight? Be sure to follow through on any of those promises. Forget, and you risk losing that client forever – people want to work only with professionals who deliver on their promises.

At the very least, after the open house, be sure to compile a summary of your open house guests for the listing agent. The preferred method is to send an email with the number of groups that came through the house and what each person thought of the home. If any guests came with their agent, be sure to tell the listing agent so that *she* can contact that agent and thank them. Likewise, if they said they are working with an agent, give that agent's name to the listing agent so *she* can follow up for an offer. Be sure to write this summary in a way that can be easily forwarded to the seller from the listing agent (refrain from non-constructive, negative comments on your behalf – if the listing agent forgets to edit those out, you will have one hurt seller on your hands!). Cut the feedback portion of the sign-in sheet and scan those in to the listing agent (you keep the contact information section for yourself) – this does not preclude you from having to write a summary about the guests! Your summary will be much more detailed than the feedback forms and is a valuable tool for the listing agent when they speak with their eager seller about the open house. Think of the summary as your thank-you to the listing agent for allowing you the business-building opportunity with their listing!

You've put in a long, hard day of work, so after you've completed the above, do yourself a favor and take the rest of the night off!

Monday: The Last Day of Your Open House Week

Mondays are to agents what the weekends are to other professionals. This is the day real estate agents tend to take the most time for themselves. Most of their clients are slammed at work, catching up after the weekend, so it's a great day for agents to recover from their busy weekend and focus on themselves.

I'm going to interfere with that time just a little bit, though. Each Monday, block one to two hours for *your business* so you can wrap up your open house week and take your open house success rate up to a whole new level.

During this hour you are going to do the following:

⇨ Write thank-you notes to everyone that attended your open house or that allowed you to put a directional in their yard. Refer back to your notes and make your letter personal to *them*. If they mentioned having a sick cat, send them well wishes. If they wanted the name of your bakery, add a business card (or a gift card!) to the bakery in your letter. They most likely visited more than one open house during the weekend. Set yourself apart from the competition by adding this personal touch.

I suggest using beautiful note cards that they'll want to keep around their house. If you use a note card that just has your company's logo on the front, the card will soon find the trash can and your 'stickability' has dwindled. Stickability is the longevity in their minds that you want to create. If you haven't stuck around in their minds, chances are pretty slim they'll reach out to you when they are ready to buy, sell or refer.

Make sure you get the thank-you letters in the mail *today* – capitalize on the relationship you began building yesterday by not allowing lag time between when they hear from you next.

⇨ For potential buyers: if they were not someone you set up to receive listing alerts from your MLS system last night, get them set up now.

You can set up every potential buyer that gave you an email address, even the ones who were not forthcoming with their wants and needs. If they didn't tell you specifically what they are looking for in a home, send them alerts on listings from the neighborhood that you held open. Now the hope is that they contact you to tailor the search to meet their criteria, and your conversations will continue from that point.

Also, be sure to send out any other data that you think they may find helpful – such as school reports, buyer resources, and the link to your blog that you wrote about the neighborhood.

⇨ For potential sellers: if you did not set up a pre-listing appointment, do a quick CMA based on the knowledge you have on their home from tax records and previous MLS listings. Let them know that this is a rough draft and that you can provide them with more specific comp values after you've seen their home.

You can also set these sellers up in your database management system to send them neighborhood comp values each month. Perhaps they won't be ready to sell until six months from now, or they are waiting for the market to heat up – either way, be the agent in front of them when they are ready!

⇨ Announce the winner for your drawing. You can really make this part fun! For the social media savvy, I suggest making a video of you drawing the names out of a bucket and posting it to your business page on Facebook. In fact, you can buddy up with someone else at your office and take turns shooting the videos for each other on Monday mornings. You don't have to be high tech with this video – a simple 20-second video will suffice.

> Be sure to tag anyone that wins, if their Facebook settings allow businesses to tag.

The video is a fantastic way to get your personality across to potential leads on your Facebook business page. You can even lure people to your page at the open house by telling them to check for the winner on your page on

Monday – a great way to get more page likes! Link the video to your website and send it out in your emails to all the visitors you had at your open house – really utilize the power of this video!

Tip: Even if you only had one person come to your open house, the video doesn't need to show that! Have several strips of paper in the bucket with the same name on each strip – or use an opaque bucket! Don't let the number of guests dictate whether or not you use this cool social media tool – it can be effective with 1 – 100 guests!

Follow the rules in your jurisdiction on drawings and giveaways and make any applicable disclosures if necessary.

Be sure to also call/email the winner to let them know the good news. See if they'll meet you for coffee instead of you simply mailing the gift card – this will give you another chance to interact and connect!

Do you have more than one guest that you felt a great connection with, but didn't win the drawing? Budget-allowing, send consolation prizes to those people as well! This could mean $5 or $10 gift cards to your favorite coffee shop – or if you remember them saying they love to take their kids out for ice cream, make it personal by giving them a gift card to an ice cream shop. You can even add the consolation prizes to your video!

Creating Long-Term Momentum from Each Open House

Those are your Monday morning steps, but the people you contacted throughout the week, and that you met at the open house, aren't done hearing from you yet! Your goal is to create a long-term relationship with each person in your open house database. Each person must be added to your mail and email database that you are ideally contacting *at least* once a month.

Remember to keep an "open house farm" for each address you hold open. This way, you can easily send out updates, such as when the house sells – a credibility-building reason to contact this specific portion of your database!

After the house has sold, and with the listing agent's permission, send postcards or letters to the homes in your open house farm: *"Our firm sold your neighbor's home, let me show you how I can sell yours, too!"*

Since you are holding open houses in an area you are farming, there will be some overlap of the addresses that you are regularly contacting. These people should receive open house invites, updates on sold homes, and other farming pieces from you on a regular basis. When they see your farming material and they see your open house material, you are confirmed in their mind as the go-to agent in the neighborhood. This is a powerful system for building your credibility as *the* neighborhood expert!

Open houses should be viewed as independent from one another in terms of short-term success. However, it is the long-term momentum of open houses that will build your credibility as the neighborhood expert. When the proper strategy is implemented, your open house leads will far succeed 160 per year.

To recap, even after the open house you must cultivate your database through contacting leads that you've met throughout the week and at the open house. Your credibility as the neighborhood expert will multiply throughout the year. Before you know it, money will flow to you from the buyers you meet, sellers who are attracted to your marketing efforts and that you've built rapport and credibility with, and people you may not even know will send you referrals because you are known as the neighborhood expert.

Now, rest up, tomorrow is Tuesday and it'll be time to select your next open house!

Key Notes:

⇨Set aside time after each open house for buyer or listing appointments with guests you meet during the day.

⇨Don't forget to pick up your signs!

⇨Be sure to follow up with anyone you made a promise to do so during your open house.

⇨Mondays are great days to follow-up with your thank-you letters and other forms of contact.

⇨The more reasons you have to reach out to your open house leads, the more you can stick in their minds.

⇨Utilize social media and videos.

⇨Have an organized database management system so no lead goes to waste.

⇨Don't forget about your leads and new database members – contact them again when the house sells or if there are price changes. Become their go-to source of information.

CHAPTER 10:

OPEN HOUSE DUTIES FOR LISTING AGENTS

This book is written to guide agents in their open houses that are other agents' listings. I'd like to address the additional steps that listing agents should take to market their open houses, whether or not they are the one holding it open.

In fact, if you are the listing agent and open house agent, you can follow every single one of the steps listed in previous chapters. You probably won't need to tour the home Tuesday and may already have a blog written about the neighborhood, otherwise your steps can be the same – and then some.

For open house agents who are not the listing agent, you will want to skip the following steps during your work week, for they are steps that only benefit the listing agent. However, you should know these steps for when you do have a listing.

Marketing

On Tuesday, enter your open house into the MLS system as soon as you confirm the date and time with the seller and the open house agent. Have a list of all the sites that advertise your listing but may not have a syndication agreement with your MLS system, and be sure to add the open house to those (for example, Realtor.com should automatically show your open house, but you may need to manually add it to Zillow or Trulia). On many virtual tour systems, there is also a spot to add your open house date and time.

Be sure that the open house agent puts an 'Open Sunday' rider in the yard; you want them to attract traffic just as badly as they do. In fact, give them a copy of this book so you can be sure that the open house is done correctly!

You will also want to run ads on Facebook, Craigslist and other applicable sites in your area. Even if another agent is holding your listing open, you still want to get the benefits of advertising your listing, since those benefits help build *your* neighborhood credibility and earn leads for *you*, too. Rerun these ads on Sunday (or open house day) morning.

If your region has a secret or closed agents-only Facebook group, post your open house there as well. This helps attract buyers' agents to your listing – and be sure to let them know they can confidently send their clients by to your professionally-held open house.

And, since it is highly probable that another agent will be the one bringing you a buyer, send out an eFlyer to area agents, announcing the open house. Your goal is to grab the attention of buyers' agents so that they think, *"Hey, where has this house been? I need to bring/send my buyer by!"* I've seen many homes go under contract because these eFlyers and agent-to-agent Facebook posts allow agents to think outside-the-box for their clients and find a house match that they normally wouldn't have seen.

Agents are inundated with emails *every* day, so your subject line must be attention-grabbing to increase the chances of the email being read. An email with a poor subject line is a waste of your time and money.

Bad example: Open House this Sunday

Good example: Stunning Elmwood House, 1.5 that Feels Like Single-Story, $445K!

Notice how I didn't even mention the open house in the subject line? Many eFlyer programs limit you on characters in the subject line, so I need to attract the right agents with my subject line and then if it appeals to them, they'll learn about the open house in the body of the email. Trust me, agents aren't waiting around for emails to learn about open houses! My goal with this subject line is to grab agents who think they have a client interested in Elmwood – a stunning home in Elmwood, not a fixer-upper – and potentially did not see this home before because their client tends to like single-story homes. I want them to realize this 1.5-story might be suitable, and if it is in their right price range ($445,000), they will bring/send their client by the open house. (And, while you have to forgo complete grammatical correctness for these space-limited subject lines, don't throw all grammar rules out the window!)

Although you will most likely leave the open house invites (either the letters or the door-to-door flyers) to the open house agent, you can still take advantage of using your listing to build neighborhood credibility through sending postcards announcing the open house, or a blanket "Call me to see the next open house date!" postcard if your postcard printer takes more than a week. It is also typical that when it comes to the bigger-budget advertising avenues, such as print newspaper ads and magazine ads, the listing agent will be the one in charge, not the open house agent who is hoping to meet buyers.

Holding Your Listing Open

If you're choosing to hold your listing open yourself, select an agent in your office that you would enjoy working with. Let him know about your open house and give him details about the house. Ask him if he would agree to a referral fee in case you come across an unrepresented buyer at your open house who wants to write an offer on your listing and would like representation. 99.9% of the agents will say yes.

Now you know who to contact on the spot when you have a buyer ready to go. Something much larger is also at work here – you're establishing a referral source with another agent. They will appreciate this and will think of you next time *they* need to find an agent to refer business to! Other agents are great sources of referrals!

When visitors come to your open house, be sure to be upfront with them that you are the listing agent. Some people have come to expect hopeful buyer agents at the open house and may rattle off information they normally wouldn't want the listing agent to know – such as that they would be willing to offer above list price on the house. Stay out of hot water by offering full disclosure up front.

You also want to be sure you still have your listing agent cap on during the open house. Unless you've been given permission in writing from your seller, you cannot release information such as if the seller would take less than the listed sales price. Remember, you are there to represent your *seller's* best interests, not the buyer's.

With these few additional steps, remember that your goals are the same as any other open house agent. You want to grow your database, generate leads and establish yourself as the neighborhood expert.

Consider doing an open house next week in the same area but that is not your listing. This way, you spread yourself out over other homes that you don't represent and you get the buyer-side of the transactions – or even run into potential buyers for your listings!

Side note: If you are owner/agent, I highly recommend you have another agent hold your listing open. At the very least, make sure you give full disclosure that you are owner/agent with all of your guests.

Key Notes:

⇨Your marketing must be attention-grabbing!

⇨Leverage yourself through holding other's listings open.

CHAPTER 11:

THE MORE THE MERRIER

Shopping malls are popular because people know that they can shop at a multitude of stores all in one trip. Whole days are sometimes dedicated to a mall trip. While it is difficult to get out of a mall without spending money on *something*, there are some days where a mall just facilitates something to do and no purchase is made.

Stand-alone boutique stores are the opposite. People visit boutiques on less occasions, though with specific reasons in mind (such as looking for a special gift or because the boutique carries a unique item) that most times result in a purchase.

These two examples are much like open houses. Like a boutique, the open house in a desolate area, with no other open houses nearby, tend to attract fewer, more serious buyers. On the other hand, people flock to popular subdivisions every Sunday morning because they are guaranteed at least a handful of open houses to check out, much like a mall. These people know their time viewing homes will be well-spent – regardless if they are serious buyers or not.

Therefore, the more open houses a community has to offer, the more people, and potential leads, you will attract to those open houses.

As a buyer's agent, use this knowledge when planning an open house. Know that your time is wisely spent when you are holding an open house in your farmed area. If that area is more desolate, that is fine because you will encounter more serious leads. What I advise you against is shying away from areas that already have other open houses, fearful of competition. I can guarantee you that not every other agent out there will do their open house the same way you do. People will naturally connect with you at times, and with other agents at other times. This is okay and this is good, because *the more the merrier*!

As a listing agent, this is powerful knowledge, especially in a slow market. Any time I have a listing 'sit', I put together a neighborhood-wide open house and homes begin to move!

The Neighborhood-Wide Open House

The neighborhood-wide open house (NWOH) uses the "more attracts more" theory, just like the mall. Even if your listing is in a neighborhood where open house activity is typically low, or in a desolate area, this strategy works.

For a NWOH, contact *all* the listing agents in the community and any FSBOs and introduce them to the thought of something larger than a typical open house – a NWOH on an event-level to attract a more-than-usual amount of buyers. Of course, when you contact the FSBO, you want to be sure they know this is *your* initiative and that you are here to help *all* sellers in the area – when that FSBO gives up working on their own, you'll be the first on their list to call (and you've added them to your database of course!).

You typically want to schedule the NWOH a couple of weeks out, to help gain momentum from other agents and the community. See which agents are on board for a reward system – for example, a stamp card that encourages visitors to rack up points for visiting every open house on the list. This helps everyone have a successful open house. Each agent can have their own drawing based on the visitors that leave their filled stamp card at their listing, or you can all decide to chip in on a grand prize for one winner.

Create a flyer with all the participating open houses and email it to the participating agents for them to get the buzz going around their office and encourage them to use it in other marketing avenues. Combined participation and advertising efforts are much more impactful than if you were the only one doing and marketing an open house.

If there is a community center or park, ask your favorite lender and other vendors to sponsor the NWOH and supply food or entertainment at the community center – you want to create an event vibe much larger than a simple open house weekend. In Austin, we have lenders who have their own radio show, so I've had them talk about my particular NWOH on their show and tell people to come to the event for free BBQ (which they sponsored) – one NWOH in particular turned into the biggest event the community had ever seen!

Because I am able to get more agents excited about a NWOH, we all tend to spend more money marketing, including newspaper ads. This is another case where I think newspaper ads are money well-spent.

Take it upon yourself to be the agent who walks the neighborhood with flyers, or sends the mail invites. Continue marketing as if you would any other time you have an open house – your goals are the same. If other agents are doing the same, good for them and you; if they are not, good for you! You are all working together to attract more buyers to your community, and there is power in numbers.

I've found that these NWOHs attract buyers in a special way to stagnant communities. The event vibe of the NWOH creates an appeal to the community that may have been lacking before, causing more buyers to consider living there. People want to live where other people like to live – even if they are social hermits, it makes them feel as though they are making a wise investment decision.

At listing appointments in communities where I have done NWOHs, or where I feel they would be effective, I am sure to mention that I coordinate activities like the NWOH and this always impresses my soon-to-be clients. They are wowed by my leadership skills, my involvement in their community and that I employ strategies to help move stagnant listings. Make this strategy your own and use power of the NWOH to move your listings faster and show off your prowess as a listing agent and the neighborhood expert.

Key Notes:

⇨Buyers are more likely to visit open houses either when a) there is a specific home they are already interested in or b) they know they will be able to view multiple homes all in a day.

⇨Stale neighborhoods benefit greatly from NWOHs.

⇨Treat NWOHs as a community event, go the extra mile with your marketing.

⇨Personally invite FSBOs.

⇨Talk about your NWOH strategy at listing appointments.

CHAPTER 12:

SAFETY FIRST

I would be remiss to write you a book about open houses without discussing the subject of safety. Anytime you are doing an open house, or showing homes to strangers, safety needs to be on the forefront of your mind.

Sadly, agents and open houses are targets for criminals – and for many reasons. Criminals tend to picture agents as wealthy people who dress expensively and drive high-end vehicles. (I hear all you newer or struggling agents laughing at this, but once you're using the techniques you learn in this book, you'll be able to afford to step up your image, too!) Criminals see agents as sitting ducks in an open house – and you've advertised how they can find you. And, what other time do they have such easy access to a home for burglary than an open house?!

In order to not fall prey, you must first be on your

151

toes and alert to your surroundings. If something does not look right to you or your gut instinct is telling you to run, then get out of the house. You are safer outside than inside 'protecting' the house. Have your phone on you at all times so that you can dial 911.

This is the reason why I discreetly watch for my open house guests to arrive. I make sure that no one sees me looking through the window (wouldn't that be a creepy sight!), by getting into a position where I can see them but they cannot see me. This way, if I sense someone with the wrong intentions is coming to the front door, I can get to the back door before they do – or even lock the front door before they reach it.

Criminals tend to attack people who are alone, so they will most likely wait until there are no other open house visitors. But be aware of the ones who wait until you are distracted with other guests to rummage through the seller's medicine cabinet and jewelry box. This is why I like to pop around from guest to guest during open houses – so everyone feels like I can be right behind them at any moment.

Speaking of behind – that is exactly where you want to be at all times with your guests: behind them. Make them enter bedrooms and stairways first. You don't want to crowd bedrooms anyway by being that extra person in the room, so stay in doorways for safety and proper house-showing reasons. When in a two-story home, I rarely go to the second story to check on my guests and usually call to them halfway up the stairs to see if they have any questions for me about the home.

Use a buddy system – whether that means you have another agent, lender or assistant with you or it means that you have someone at your office that knows your whereabouts and you have check-in times. However, do not feel overconfident if there are two of you at the open house. Unfortunately criminals do get bold and have attacked two agents at an open house before. The same applies for you burly men – you are just as much at risk as any other agent when it comes to being alone in an open house.

Talk to your local law enforcement officials to learn what type of protection devices you can carry, such as pepper spray, or even look into concealed handgun licensing. Get together with agents in your office and take a self-defense class.

Educate the sellers on removing any items of value, medications and weapons; although criminals have been known to steal clothes and everyday household items.

Open houses, like meeting new buyers to show properties, are an important to your well-balanced real estate career, so do not let the fear of being attacked get in your way of success. Instead, be on alert and have a plan in place in case something does go awry.

Key Notes:

⇨Always be alert and carry your charged phone with you.

⇨Educate your sellers on hiding their prized possessions.

⇨Let guests enter rooms before you; be careful about following them upstairs.

⇨Use a buddy system.

⇨Don't let fear get in the way of your success. Prepare yourself instead so that it is less likely to catch you off-guard.

CHAPTER 13:

IMPLEMENTATION EQUALS SUCCESS

I hope that up to this point you've highlighted and dog-eared all the open house strategies in this book and you are feeling confident in your ability to have a successful open house. Be sure to also check out the free resources that accompany this book at: www.ShannonEnsor.com/yktohs/resources.

I love the aha moment on agent's faces when they realize that open houses are more than just sitting in a house and hoping a buyer comes along. When they understand that open houses build their neighborhood credibility, bring them leads from the open house *and* their marketing efforts, and help them grow their database from the farming aspect to the visitors, they make it a priority in their well-rounded real estate career. It becomes one of their favorite "pieces of the real estate pie"!

Knowing that open houses attract more than buyers – that visitors can also be people slyly interviewing agents for listing their home or for a referral for a family member that is moving to the area – helps agents to have a wider perspective when they are meeting open house guests.

With the combination of online marketing and neighborhood marketing, you are armed to find great success with your open houses. But, the most important success key with open houses is to actually *do them*. You can't just think about open houses and expect for them to make you money. Remember, you have to be in the open house game to win.

The more open houses you have, the higher your database numbers will climb and the higher your annual income will rise. **Start this very next Tuesday and schedule your open house for the weekend!**

I wish you success at each and every one of your open houses!

With Gratitude

I dedicate this book to my handsome hubby who has unselfishly accompanied me to every open house I've ever done. He has spent many hours sweating in the Texas sun, putting out directional signs and chasing down errant balloons. His assistance helped me fine-tune my methods and we helped each other grow into better agents because of our countless open houses together.

Thank you from the bottom of my heart for all that you have done, Joe!

About the Author

Shannon Ensor has been an Austin REALTOR and broker since 2005. In addition to being a top-producing agent, she coaches and mentors a team of agents. One day, while creating a guide on open houses for her team, Shannon realized she had enough information and strategies to fill a book! Thus, *Your Key to Open House Success* was born. Carrying on her desire to teach and help other agents become successful, she filled the book with every secret, strategy and tactic she had learned over her years of building a successful business through open houses. In mentoring agents, Shannon has also learned the go-to objections agents create that sabotage their success. She passes along her sabotage-proof mindset to her readers and hopes that each one will gain the knowledge and motivation to become the best agent they can possibly be.

www.ShannonEnsor.com

www.facebook.com/ShannonEnsorBooks

Made in the USA
Coppell, TX
27 July 2021